CON.ＫUVERSY

Sex, Lies and Dirty Money By The World's Powerful Elite - Volume I

Ian Halperin

PRZ Publishing

CONTENTS

SEX, LIES AND DIRTY
MONEY BY THE WORLD'S
POWERFUL ELITE

Volume I: A Royal Rumble
by Ian Halperin
#1 NY Times Bestselling Author

AUTHOR'S NOTE

Jeffrey Epstein's impact on the world has been profound - all in the most negative way. His controversial rise and fall has left many A-list celebrities linked to him shaking in their boots, fearing the day their true involvement with the notorious sociopath would finally be exposed. The wild, terrifying level-3 registered sex offender led a Dr. Jekyll-Mr. Hyde life for decades, a life even the most demented Hollywood scriptwriters could not have dreamed of. His atrocious behavior is too dangerous a force to await the final judgment of the dozens of lingering sexual abuse cases against the dead pedophile's estate.

With a six volume book series CONTROVERSY, I attempt to chronicle the abuse of power by the world's richest people. There is no better way to start than to delve into the misogynistic, barbaric life of the despicable New York wealthy financial advisor/ sex offender who drove the world to the brink of chaos by committing a countless number of horrific sex crimes. He used his network of famous friends and acquaintances like Prince Andrew, Bill Clinton, Donald Trump, Woody Allen and Ghislaine Maxwell to help expand his international child sex trafficking ring.

A major focus of this first volume is to examine the gross abuse of power and deceit by people connected to royalty, including Epstein, The British Royal Monarchy and a slew of other well known members of royal families around the world. I also delve into several famous people's lifelong obsessions with linking themselves to royalty. The self absorbed American icons who profess to be royalty, even though the U.S. has not been part of the British empire for hundreds of years, includes The Queen of Pop - Madonna, the self proclaimed King Of All Media Howard Stern and basketball icon King Lebron James.

The vast majority of the material in this book is taken from more than six hours of conversations I had when I interviewed Epstein. At the time, I had no idea he would become the world's most notorious sex offender. Between 2001 and 2020 I interviewed more than 600 people connected to the deranged sociopath. Most of the interviews took place in person. Another 137 people I contacted declined to participate. Some of the people in the book asked to be sourced using a pseudonym because they feared a backlash if their real names were to be revealed. No-one was sourced in this book without undergoing a deep background check. I should warn that not all the conversations I have described here are verbatim recordings. With the help of all these sources, I have reconstructed some of the dialogue with extreme sensitivity and care. Where my memory didn't recollect perfectly, I have left out quotation marks.

I am indebted to those sources who were brave enough to go on the record and am extremely grateful to two of Epstein's close associates who granted me hours of interviews in exchange for complete anonymity.

I could have not written this without the co-operation of several key people in Epstein's inner circle who granted me exclusive, never before revealed information about him; especially how the demented sociopath operated. One key person closely connected to Epstein who agreed to give me an interview suddenly pulled out a day before we were scheduled to meet. To this day I have never heard back from him. All his contact information have changed. Many people connected to Epstein have told me they think it's not just some strange co-incidence and that someone forced him to go silent - or made him disappear.

I rely on forensic pathological evidence and key people connected to Epstein to attempt to get to the bottom surrounding the mystery of how the former Wall Street billionaire died. I interviewed many credible people in his inner circle who concluded that there were people who wanted Epstein out of the way. In fact, one source revealed that Epstein told him just weeks before his death that he was worried for his safety and feared there were people out there who were planning to kill him..

There have been numerous books and films that have done a great job uncovering the sordid details of Epstein's life, combining the intricate facts surrounding the multitude of court cases launched against his estate . Although I rely on archival information for background information, my focus is not to rehash what is already published. Instead, I attempt to chronicle the never-before-revealed details I learned first hand from the hundreds of contacts I cultivated that were connected to Epstein in the modeling world, Hollywood and Wall Street. I made those contacts over 20 years, having written 18 books and directed several documentaries which deal for the most part with corruption, tragedy, abuse and prejudice in the entertainment industry.

This book is a deep and painful journey with extremely sensitive and alarming material. Above everything, it is dedicated to all the brave victims who find the courage to speak out against the inhuman suffering and abuse that was thrown on them by a severely dangerous, wealthy, egomaniac, sociopath who ran a highly sick and sadistic sex trafficking ring.

CHAPTER I - MOLDING
THE MANIAC

Midtown Manhattan, late fall season 2001 - 12:07pm. I'm sitting in a booth toward the back of the iconic Benash Deli on 7th and West 55th Street. The schmutzy walls are covered with celebrity photos and tacky fifties memorabilia. The eastern european aroma of pastrami, matzah ball soup and baked knishes permeate the entire restaurant. Benash, which opened in 1990, is one of New York City's iconic delis. There are few things New Yorkers crave more than a ginormous pastrami sandwich with a side of pumpernickel, pickles and coleslaw. The chicken soup I ordered was out-of-this-world delicious. "We live in a society based on instant gratification," the grey haired, bespectacled fifty something waitress told me in a thick NY accent. "That's why this place is so packed all the time. I've seen stars like Johnny Carson, Regis Philbin, Puff Daddy and Whitney Houston all come in here. We've had them all - falling stars, mobsters, hookers, bankers, multi millionaires and cops come here with different types of palates. By the time they're done they all leave satisfied and come back for more usually a day or two later. The food is that good here." By the time the waitress and I finish kibitzing the person I'm here to meet finally shows up. Clearly he's a regular at Benash as the waitress and him exchanged pleasantries. "How's your day going?," he said to her. "Always good to see you. You're the best."

This man, a renowned Wall Street money manager, agreed to meet me at the behest of a mutual friend we had. This would be my second time meeting Epstein. He didn't seem to recognize me from the first meeting so I didn't bring it up. It was dark when I initially met him on a rooftop bar so it's understandable he didn't recognize me. He was also in a party mood, seeming slightly intoxicated, and in a jolly mood being around so many beautiful models.

A couple of years prior when I met him he was partying with a bunch of leggy models who were young enough to be his daughter. I had a conversation with him that night which turned out to be key information for a book I'd get published a couple years later. He knew everything about the dark side of the modeling business, and on this night was more than willing to talk about it. "All the models who do heroin they hide the track marks by injecting needles under their toenails," he told me. "Every model does coke or heroin. That's how they stay so thin."

He bragged about all the beautiful women around him and all the beautiful models he knew, and told me that a London stripclub owner was his idol. "Peter Stringfellow is my hero." he said. "He's made millions being around naked girls every day. Not many guys in this world can say that. What a life he's had." Before the end of the night, this master egomaniac would give me some key inside scoops on the industry I was about to infiltrate. Epstein's deep connections and knowledge of the modeling business turned out to be extremely valuable in my research. In my book I quoted him off-the-record.

Waiting can be a great humbler. And that's why I believe he kept me waiting more than forty five minutes after the time we were supposed to meet. If he hadn't shown up by the time I was done with my chicken soup I would have left. He sat down, exchanged small talk before we finally got started on the matter at hand.

From the get go he seemed slightly wary of opening up to me but was very present, elaborating on everything I brought up. The idea to interview the man who would become the world's most dangerous sex offender first happened in late fall 2001, barely a couple months after the sadness, shock and horror of the appalling terrorist attacks of 911. It was around that time I was able to interview, through a mutual friend connection, a slim, athletic salt and pepper 6 foot New York financier who gave me the dirt on an industry renowned for abusing girls in their early teens. He was supposed to turn out to be one of my key sources for a book I wrote infiltrating the fashion industry, Bad&Beautiful, by posing undercover as a male model. But there were two problems: 1) that chilling late fall day he talked about everything one could imagine but barely brushed over what I had come for - to get the dirt on the perils of the modeling industry. 2) My book had already been printed so I was hoping to get key information from him for the updated paperback which was scheduled to be released a couple months later. I had no inkling the charming, suave, outspoken Epstein one day would become so famous - but for atrocious reasons.

For years, I made my name posing undercover, infiltrating institutions such as Hollywood, The Church of Scientology and the music industry. In return for an interview the slick, imposing man made me agree to pay a price - to guarantee him complete anonymity. Everything, he insisted, had to be attributed to an unnamed source. "If you ever betray my confidence I'll make sure your life will be just about over," he said looking me straight in the face showing off his piercing blue eyes. "I'll give you everything you need. I know all the key players. I've fucked the hottest models in the world. I chew them up and spit them out before they realize they were the flavor of the day for me - but I know they enjoy the taste I leave in their mouth. Because of me your book will become a huge bestseller. But don't fuck with me. I'm not one to be played." Ironically, most of the stuff he told me this second meeting would be useless to me until years later when he became so famous. I already used the stuff he told me two years ago in the book's first edition. For the upcoming paperback he didn't provide much of anything new. It was evident he was in the mood to go on and on about anything and everything, except about what I came for. Years later I'd learn he did it on purpose, going in circles to make me dizzy in order to make sure I wouldn't expose him in the book. He told a friend he thought I was out to "lift the lid" on him. Although he basically threatened me if I outed him, it seemed he wanted to make sure he didn't give me anything remotely associated about his wild forays with stunning models. It was a complete contrast to the first time I met him two years ago when when he couldn't stop bragging about all the models he slept with and was more than willing to out the modeling industry's key players. During that first interview, however, I didn't introduce myself as a journalist.

The contrasts between Epstein and your stereotypical Wall Street executive were quite evident. He dressed casually, in a black sports shirt and pants, a pair of running shoes, disheveled hair and he didn't seem at all bothered by the dingy atmosphere of Benash. "I love this place," he told me. "Usually I eat healthy or fine dining but when I need to eat bubby food I come here. It brings me back to my roots."

Epstein grew up in SeaGate, a predominantly Jewish middle class neighborhood on the Western edge of Coney Island. His parents, Seymour and Paula, were the children of European immigrants. Seymour worked for the city as a gardener and trash collector while Paula worked as a school aide. Paula was also a role model homemaker, always maintaining a happy, clean home.

"They were a humble, hard working quiet family," said Eileen Nussbaum, a former neighbor of Epstein. "They never caused any trouble. And they were always very kind. I did find young Jeffrey to be a bit mysterious, very isolated and having a strange energy. He was an enigma ever since I met him. I lived a few houses down the street. One time while I was in my bathroom I caught him peeking through my bathroom window trying to get a glimpse of me getting my four year old daughter prepared for a bath. When he saw I noticed him in the backyard peeking in he ran off faster than a speeding bullet. Another time I caught him lurking around the side of our home trying to peek into my oldest daughter's room. She was seven at the time. She started crying hysterically that someone was trying to peek in on her. When I rushed to her room I made eye contact with Jeffrey again. One more time he ran off - faster than I had ever seen him run. It never happened again and I didn't think much of it until many years later when I read about his terrible behavior in the newspapers. It was then I put two and two together."

Epstein's parents encouraged him and his younger brother Mark to pursue their dreams, no matter what they were. "Jeffrey was interested in art and numbers, ever since I remember him as a young, shy boy," said David, a longtime family friend who asked that his last name not be published. "Mark on the other hand was a bit more outgoing. He was more talkative and liked to play with his friends. I rarely saw Jeffrey play with friends, especially friends his own age. I remember one time I met him and Seymour at the local playground and Seymour told Jeffrey to go play for a bit cause Seymour wanted to talk to me about a business idea he had. There were plenty of kids his own age in the park but Jeffrey ended up playing in the sandbox with a girl who couldn't have been over three years old. He was making small sandcastles with her while her mother watched from a few feet away. I remember having a strange feeling about it then. It just seemed a bit strange and a bit weird that Jeffrey who was around

9 back then didn't play with kids who were his own age. Young Jeffrey's actions even gained more resonance with David when Seymour told David that day that his enigmatic son had an aversion to playing with kids who weren't much younger than him. "I remember when he told me that," David said. "I found it to be so weird. Something didn't feel quite right."

Both Mark and Jeffrey were keen on developing their skills in the art world but were also very interested in finance. They wanted to become rich. Jeffrey was a student prodigy, a mathematics wiz, having skipped two grades before attending Lafayette High School in Brooklyn. He tutored math on the side and from an early age had the ambition to make lots of money. He wanted to have a better life than the one he grew up in with his parents. It was either he adapted to a life as a struggling pianist or to make a ton of money pursuing a career in finance. He chose the latter.

"He was one of the most talented young concert pianists in the New York area," a former classmate said. "We called him Eppy. He was a bit hard to figure out but in general the students liked him. He became popular even though he seemed to be a bit mysterious. He never showed too much emotion. Some of the students thought it was all part of him being somewhat of a genius - a piano prodigy who excelled in math. That's a very powerful one-two punch when you're young. It commanded him instant respect among his fellow classmates."

At Lafayette, Epstein earned his way on the

school's math team. He excelled in every subject except history. It was a subject he found difficult to apply himself. One of his former classmates recalled him falling asleep during class. "He seemed to be in another world, completely withdrawn," said "Sarah", who requested her real name not be used for publication. "It was common knowledge back then that he was great at math and music. But in other subjects he wasn't close to being at the top of the class. He was a total enigma. Some of the girls were attracted to him because he did possess more charm than the average guy at school. But he didn't return the interest. In fact, I know for a fact he was interested in a girl two grades below him and apparently they were once caught making out in the girl's washroom. He got caught there and was reprimanded by his teacher and almost got suspended from school."

Epstein attended Cooper Union and New York University but never graduated with a degree. Still, in 1974, he managed to get a job teaching math and physics at the esteemed Dalton prep school in Manhattan. Donald Barr was Dalton's headmaster at the time — a man who was known for being strict, imposing and extremely conservative. He's the father of the Trump administration's Attorney General William Barr. As the nation's highest law enforcement officer, Barr was leading the charge in prosecuting Epstein after he'd been arrested again.

"The joke has been this is the Epstein-Barr problem at Dalton," said Harry Segal, a senior lecturer at Cornell University and Weill Cornell Medical

College who graduated from Dalton in 1974. The Epstein-Barr virus, which is a type of herpes that can cause mono, ironically bears the name of the men who were the main players in the scandal that shook up Dalton. Another source said Barr was keen to go all out to throw the book at Epstein. "He was determined to make sure Epstein got the most severe penalty possible," a source who worked on the case revealed. "He didn't want the media or his critics saying he went light on Epstein because of the link to his father. He was very determined to bury Epstein."

Quickly, Epstein became a regular topic of conversation among the students - but for all the wrong reasons. Many students talked about the unorthodox way he dressed, especially for the role of teacher. He'd walk into class decked out in bright pants, open shirt, gold chains and leather boots.

"He looked more like a pimp in Times Square than a math teacher," a former female student of his said. "He had a roving eye for young girls. When he was in front of the class teaching he'd look at me occasionally, glancing at my chest. He'd stare in that direction for a few seconds before turning my head. One time I caught him staring at my friends' ass when she got up to go to the bathroom. Looking back I now realize he was a complete pig.

"One girl in my class bragged back then that she once went to his apartment and had sex with him. We thought she was making it up. She said they had sex for hours and that she took a taxi home the next morning, telling her worried parents she had fallen asleep at a girlfriends' house. There were rumors of Epstein having several affairs with both teachers and students. He was a big topic of conversation back then. He tried to play the part of a math teacher but his persona dictated otherwise. He was more of a player than a teacher - a man obsessed with his physical appearance who craved the attention of all the females in the room. It was quite disturbing."

The amateurishness of his teaching methods combined with the anarchic atmosphere Epstein displayed in front of his students led to his dismissal in 1976 by the head of the school Peter Branch, who would later explain in an interview his reasons for sacking Epstein. He was most clear. "It was determined that he had not adequately grown as a new teacher to the standard of the school." Furthermore, it was discovered that Epstein lied on his job application to the school. He embellished his credentials and lied about his academic achievements. This would set the stage for the manner in which Epstein would lead the rest of his life; a professional conman/ pathological liar who could lie his way out of just about anything.

"He made seasoned pros like Bernie Madoff and Roger Stone look like amateurs," said Stanley Hill, a former Wall Street associate of Epstein. "Epstein was a professional con man at the highest level. Everything he did from financial management to luring innocent, underage girls from all over the world was based on lies. We've seen some characters in America who are more crooked than a dog's hind leg. But Epstein was in a league of his own. He was the type of guy who everyone just wanted to believe, even if they were being taken for a ride. If anyone put the con in conniving it certainly was Epstein."

Aside from the rumors of Epstein bedding young students, he was caught partying with a bunch of female students at a party and allegedly took a weekend trip with an underage teen to the birthplace of American art - the Catskills. According to multiple sources, he spent two days there with an underage brunette, just a few years his junior. Epstein was 20 years old when he taught at Dalton. He told his students not to worry about his curriculum because he promised them they would all get A's.

"I remember my friend told me she went out of town with him for the weekend," a former student recalled. "She told me in confidence back then that she slept with him and was enamored by his charisma and charm. She claimed to be in love with him. I tried to talk her out of it but it didn't work. She kept seeing him outside of class for around a month before he decided to end it because he told her it wasn't morally right. He crushed her feelings. It took her the rest of the year to get over it. It wasn't easy for her."

Dalton alumina Scott Spizer was interviewed by the New York Times for an article about Epstein's tenure at Dalton.. "I can remember thinking at the time 'this is wrong. '"He was much more present amongst the students, specifically the girl students, during non-teaching hours...it was kind of inappropriate." Another former pupil Mark Robinson, who wasn't in Epstein's class, said other students were drawn to his unconventional teaching methods, but found his behavior outside the classroom "creepy." Robinson revealed to the U.K. Sun: "The perception of Epstein was that he was a twenty-something who preferred hanging out with teenage students and acted like them, even in school. To this day there are former students who remember Epstein showing up at student parties, hitting on young girls without any shame or remorse. "He was a complete pig," a former female student recalled. "So many rumors popped up about him having affairs with students. It was disgusting. The man was nothing more than a sick, deranged megalomaniac who was the biggest pervert I ever met. He was a conman, one who should have never been granted the opportunity to teach young students. He was sick, mentally imbalanced."

Years later, in a 2009 court deposition, Epstein denied sexually abusing any of his female students. When asked if he had sexual intercourse with any of his students at Dalton, he replied, "not that I can remember." "He's a pathological liar, always has been," a former female student at Dalton said. "It was common knowledge back then that he liked to shit where he ate. He was gross, a man with no respect for himself or anybody else. He was a very twisted man. If there was a Me Too movement back then he would have been busted immediately. He was a full time predator who's ego was bigger than Mount Everest."

One former Dalton student I tracked down now lives in **Phoenix, Arizona.** She said Epstein tried to seduce her at a party when she was sixteen. Although she refused his advances she says she felt he as if he "tried to rape me". " Just because we didn't have sex doesn't mean I wasn't abused," she said. "Physically and emotionally he took everything out of me that night. And in the process he scarred me forever. I never got over it. It stayed with me for the rest of my life.

"He was a professional sex abuser. He looked in my eyes and almost put me in a trance. He started caressing me as if I was his little puppy. For a few minutes I actually enjoyed him touching me. It felt weird but good. I almost fell into his trap, I managed to snap out of his spell at the last second. I wish I would have reported him. Maybe that would have gotten him arrested back then for sexually harassing a student and it might have stopped him from going further. Every day I think what if? It's very hard to live with."

During the course of my investigation I interviewed several models who, like the student, claim they were put under a spell by Epstein. Unlike the female student, many of them ended up in Epstein's bed. A few of them ended up being trafficked for sex by Epstein and his handlers. A former Vogue and Elle model from Paris explained to me how Epstein met her at a fashion show during New York Fashion Week and fell head over heels for her. At the time she was only 16. She said Epstein seduced her during a massage, engaging in water sports and shocking her with a golden shower.

"He came up to me after the show and worked his charm on me," she said. "The next thing I know is he's giving me a massage at his huge home that turns into the most erotic massage once could ever imagine. At one point he pulled down his pants and started massaging his penis all over my face while I lay naked on the bed. And then he peed all over my face and body. He said his pee was an antibacterial shield that would clear my chakras and relieve all toxins in my body. Even though it was disgusting, I fell for it. He peed all over me, even my feet. Then he poured edible massage oil all over my body and licked it all off. We had sex all night and I left early the next morning."

A couple days later the stunning five-foot-ten, brunette went back to Epstein's home to attend a dinner party. She says there were several friends of Epstein there, including a couple of middle aged billionaires from Saudi Arabia. At least five girls, she said, who didn't look a day over 15 were there. There was a table full of high end Italian food. The booze was flowing like water and the girls started making their way into bedrooms in the house with the middle aged male guests. According to the Paris model, all the girls were paid by Epstein $750.00 to be there for the entire night and to offer themselves to Epstein's guests. At the beginning of the evening, Epstein announced to his guests that the women were available to everyone for tips. The Paris model presumed she'd sleep with Epstein that night, especially after the steamy night they had a couple nights earlier. But she was dead wrong. Instead, Epstein offered her to one of the men from the Middle East. She tried to get up to leave but Epstein stopped her. They talked for around fifteen minutes. She broke down and cried, feeling humiliated by Epstein's thoughtless gesture. The only thing she remembers vividly is waking up naked several hours later next to the five-foot-seven inch, portly Saudi Arabian bald man who was in bed smoking a cigarette.

"It was clear they did something like drugging me with something to knock me out," she recalled. "I was raped. When I woke up the creepy man who I had met for the first time a few hours earlier was in bed next to me smoking a cigarette, reading a book as if nothing had happened. I started crying hysterically and told him I was going to call the police. He tried to calm me down. He took out two thousand dollars cash and put it in my hand. I threw the money in his face. It was at that point he got up to get his blazer, pulled another fifteen thousand dollars from his pocket and told me he'd give it to me if I didn't mention a word to anyone. That was a lot of money to me, especially at that time when I had rent and a lot of other bills coming in. Reluctantly, I agreed. I felt trafficked out by Jeffrey but what could I do. Even if I called the police I don't think they would have done a thing. I realized quickly that Jeffrey had contacts everywhere and paid people off in all key areas so that he could avoid getting into trouble. He's one person who thought he was above all laws. That's why he was able to get away with raping so many girls for so long. He had this way of making everyone live in fear, making them feel he did something wrong - not them. He was such a fucking pig!"

The model, who now lives in Ireland, said that she was sex trafficked by Epstein to clients and close friends for almost two years before having a nervous breakdown. To this day, she's still recovering. "He abused me when I was still a child - a minor," she said during a 2018 skype call. "He did everything he could to ruin my mind and my well being. He was completely controlling and a Svengali like monster. At first I thought it was easy money but as time went on he dragged me into things I never wanted to ever go near including wild orgies, going on wealthy men's boats for a few days to have sex with them and treating me as if I was a sex slave. I'm still in therapy and I don't think it's something that I can ever get over."

Well respected Miami psychiatrist and best-selling author Dr. Eva Ritvo says that child sexual abuse victims often become victims of child sex trafficking. "Victims of childhood sexual abuse have many multiple psychological sequela including Depression, Anxiety, Post-Traumatic Stress Disorder, Eating Disorders, Substance Use Disorders and more.

In extreme cases, victims of childhood sexual abuse may become victims of sex trafficking."

The French model, who asked not to be named, would be one of many women I interviewed for this book that claimed Epstein ran a sophisticated operation of drug facilitated sexual assaults on young girls whom he was able to lure to one of the many mansions he owned around the world; albeit in his palatial Avenue Foch apartment in Paris, a 40-room pad on 71st Street on New York's Upper East Side, a mansion in Florida's exclusive Palm Beach area, his sprawling Zorro ranch in New Mexico and the infamous Paedophile Island in Little St. James near St. Thomas in the Virgin Islands, On all of these properties there have been allegations of Epstein and his handlers having sex with underage girls., Many of these girls were drugged and raped while they were in an unconscious state. Epstein's intention was always the same - to do whatever was necessary to have sex with them.

Another former model from Holland that I interviewed shared the scary realities of being unwillingly forced to have sex the same night back in 2005 with Epstein and a French model agency owner. She says she hadn't yet turned 15. "I was working in Paris and they invited me out for dinner," she said. "They were plying me with drinks all night. When we left I thought they'd call me a taxi but instead dragged me into their taxi. Epstein instructed the driver to drop us off at his apartment. When we got there they gave me more alcohol. At one point

I started to feel weird and completely blacked out. To this day I'm convinced they roofied me. The next morning I woke up naked in Epstein's bed. I started to put two and two together. I was unknowingly drugged."

One of the places I spent time doing research in was the Virgin Islands, where Epstein had a 72-acre private island in Little St. James, located close to St. Thomas. I interviewed 61 people there that were connected to him. They included former employees and acquaintances. According to a former Epstein household employee I was able to track down, the sex crazed Epstein usually had a stash of designer drugs in the house to knock out his victims. She even once joked to him that he should have been in the "roofing" business. "His drug operation was much more elaborate than has been previously reported," said Debra Gale, a former housekeeper for Epstein. "There were times when he'd knock out a girl with drugs and have him and his friends take turns having sex with her. It was very terrible what he did and highly illegal. I thought of going to the police but all his staff signed NDA's. He always was above the law. I didn't want to end up in jail myself for not contacting the police. But I knew how powerful Mr. Epstein was and I was afraid he'd turn it all around on me or another staff member. So I kept my lips sealed."

Gale said she had another reason, too, for being afraid of her boss. She witnessed first hand what went on when famous people visited his mansion, the one she worked at for more than three years on the private island that he purchased for 7.95 million dollars in 1998. The property became dubbed by local "Pedophile Island" because of all the underage girls Epstein had coming in and out. The property was designed by famous designer Ed Tuttle, renowned for his work for the exclusive Aman resorts.

"You told me you're from Canada, right?," she said to me. "What part?" When I told her Montreal, Quebec her eyes lit up. "Oh my god," she responded. "I have never met bigger party animals than the people he flew in from Quebec. I was working that week when Mr. Epstein flew in a well known politician from there with a couple of businessmen and six girls who only spoke french. At least three of the girls were strippers in clubs up there, I overheard the politician saying that. It was unreal what went on. The Quebec people, including the politician, were partying so hard, almost as if the world was about to end. Mr. Epstein loved french girls, especially the ones from Quebec because he said he spent time up there when he was young. The girls were paid by Mr. Epstein to have wild orgies all week with him and his male guests. I had never seen so much sex going on in the house at one time. They went at it all day. I was privy to how it started when Mr. Epstein gave his guests the first choice of the girls they wanted. Being a good host, he chose last. There was lots of booze, drugs and food that Mr. Epstein provided for his guests. Everyone of them I saw doing cocaine during their stay, especially the politician. He liked to get high on cocaine. Not one of the guests didn't party hard. The girls were stunning. They must have all been between 16-20 years in age, not more than that. And they were all more than willing to party with the group of middle aged men who brought them to Little St. James. One morning I came into the main salon and saw the politician completely passed out on the floor with no shirt on and in his underwear. At some point he must have passed out. The next night I saw him go into one of the bedrooms with a girl who looked very young. I heard her tell Mr. Epstein that she was 19 but to me she didn't look a day over 16. And I'm usually very good at profiling people's correct ages."

Later in the book I'll reveal more about the politician and what happened during his sejour at Epstein's private island, including a first hand account of how he once partied there with Bill Clinton in the company of what one witness called "girls who looked more like children."

One city Epstein told me he found glamorous and exciting was my hometown, Montreal. When I interviewed him at Benash for my models book he bragged to me how Montreal was the city where he first started to hone his skills.

"It's the most European city in North America," he told me. "It's the city in Canada which I adore most. I love Leonard Cohen, I love the hockey team there (Montreal Canadiens), I love the cuisine which in my opinion is right up there with New York's restaurants, and I love the beautiful french women. That's the city in which I had many of my first life experiences." At the time I thought he was just talking out of his ass but later I'd learn Epstein really did learn the tricks of his "trade" in my hometown.

A few years later I'd be introduced to the man who recruited young girls for Epstein from all over the world, including Ukraine, Paris, Tokyo, Brazil and Montreal. I met him at a party in Paris during Paris Fashion Week at the trendy, posh Hotel Costes on rue St-Honore. A mutual friend from Riyadh, the capital of Saudi Arabia, introduced us. He introduced himself as Pepe. He bragged to me how he was the "billionaire" Jeffrey Epstein's "right hand guy". I told Pepe Epstein willingly was a source for a book about the fashion industry I wrote a few years ago. He seemed to be impressed. Pepe would become one of the key sources for my investigation.

With nowhere to sit in the jam packed atrium of Hotel Costes, Pepe and I went to have a drink at the bar. I found him to be warm, funny and charming. After we each ordered a glass of vodka and soda we got into deep conversation. He told me he's lived all over the world but now divided his time between Toulouse and Paris when Epstein's in town. Pepe told me Epstein owned real estate in Paris and would make frequent trips there. When I told Pepe I was originally from Montreal, he told me he once lived on the outskirts of the city with his mother when he was young and had heard a lot of wild stories about the city from Epstein.

"That's where he came into his own," Pepe told me. "If not for a trip to Montreal in 1971 when he was 18 his life would have probably turned out to be completely different. He might not have become the huge party animal he is today." I asked him to elaborate and he was more than willing to oblige. "Montreal inspired him to become a sex maniac. If not for Montreal maybe he would have become a wealthy financial advisor and a rabbi on the side instead of becoming a wealthy financier and a rapist on the side.

"He told me when he visited Montreal it was the first time he had the type of fun with a woman that prior to that he could only fantasize about," he told me. "The story goes that he ended up in some hotel downtown with three girls he met in a bar and had the first sexual experience of his life with multiple partners at the same time. He told me he became addicted to it. The next four nights he had two or three girls a night at the same time. He said he picked some up at bars and some were escorts that he hired. He told me how easy it was to pick up women in Montreal. Is that true," he asked me. When I responded Montreal was known for its beautiful women Pepe went on about Epstein's first trip there. "Jeffrey told me how open the women are there and how easy it is to go to a bar and take them back to the hotel the same night. He started going there often for several years after that. Some of the girls he picked up in the bars in Montreal were several years underage. But you know Jeffrey, he doesn't care at all."

Later in the book I'll reveal some shocking revelations about Epstein I got from Pepe, one which I think will shock the entire world. First, I want to make clear how I gained access to all these key Epstein sources. I'm a journalist who specializes in undercover investigations, having previously posed undercover as Michael Jackson's hair stylist, a a male escort in Hollywood and an alleged gay actor who joined the Church of Scientology wanting to be cured of being my alleged homosexuality.

Back in 2001 when I posed undercover as a male model to infiltrate the fashion industry to help me write a book that became an international bestseller, the book made headlines because of all the sex and drug abuse I exposed in the fashion industry. Famous novelist Jackie Collins chose it as book of the year in the year end best picks in the London Daily Mail. If not for Jackie's incredible support I most likely would have left the book business to find a real day job. Collins, who sold more than 500 million books before she died of cancer in September 2015, called the book a "a fascinating portrait". Her incredible support opened up a lot of doors for me, including getting a new literary agent and becoming a documentary filmmaker.

Infiltrating the modeling business gave me a lot of access to many of the stunning, cutting edge models strutting the catwalks in New York, London, Paris, and Milan. A lot of the contacts I cultivated in the business had links to Epstein. In fact, it was a mutual friend who used to be in the fashion business and ended up working on Wall Street that suggested I interview Epstein for the book. I knew him through his son, who was an aspiring filmmaker. "Nobody knows the business better than my good friend Jeffrey Epstein," said the former Bear Stearns junk-bond trader who first met Epstein back in the early eighties. "He'll give you all the information you need, stuff that will make your hair turn upside down. He's told me many of the stories. I'm sure he'll be more than happy to help you. He owes me a couple of favors. I helped him do some deals when we worked together that helped make him a very wealthy man."

Epstein got his first job on Wall Street through a connection of one of his former teenage female students after he got sacked at Dalton. The legendary brokerage firm Bear Stearns was run by the students' legendary day trader father, Alan "Ace" Greenberg. Lynne Greenberg convinced her Wall Street power-house father how her off the wall math teacher with movie star charm could be a good match to work at his firm. Greenberg had a penchant for hiring outside the box. Most Wall Street firms scouted top ivy league schools looking for young, bright stars. Greenberg was one of the few Wall Street executives who like to hire young, scrappy, charismatic young males with an edge who were hungry to make a good living.

"Epstein had the perfect working DNA that Greenberg was looking to hire," Schwartz said. "He was young, scrappy and had great knowledge of tax law on how the rich could avoid paying tax through investments. He quickly became Greenberg's favorite employee. Greenberg worked closely with him, turning him into the biggest rising star in the firm. Epstein wasn't afraid to take the risks that reminded Greenberg of himself when he was younger. He spent more time mentoring Epstein than anyone else at Bear Sterns."

Just a few years after leaving Dalton and his minimal teaching salary, Epstein became a junior partner at Bear Stearns. Within a short time he became a multimillionaire, earning millions in year end bonuses. But it only took a few years before his time at Bear Stearns would erupt like a volcano and burn many in his path. "There were many, many accusations against him," Schwartz revealed. "It didn't take long. Greenberg was aware that Epstein dated much younger girls and that he had a secret life. He received a couple of complaints of sexual harassment from several young female employees but he did damage control and managed to keep it hush hush. He didn't want to lose the talents of his young prodigy.

"The final straw was when Epstein got caught running up ludicrous tabs on his personal expense accounts," a former Bear Stearns colleague said. "He was billing the firm for everything from private yoga instruction to massage parlors to drinks at some of New York City's most exclusive gentlemen's clubs. He also billed the firm for airline tickets that were not used for business purposes. They were used for his own personal fun. Some of the names that appeared on the tickets were names of girls that an internal investigation revealed were strippers and escorts. Bear Stearns had no choice but to terminate his services. It was a reluctant termination because Eppy was making the firm so much money. He was a financial genius. He knew more about the financial industry than top professors at Harvard and Whartan. He was looked upon at the firm as being a financial guru."

Soon after his dismissal from Bear Stearns Epstein decided to go out on his own. He started his own money management firm that specialized in managing wealthy people's private portfolios. The biggest client at Epstein's Financial Trust Co. would turn out to be Victoria's Secret billionaire founder Leslie Wexner. Epstein devoted most of his time to working on Wexner's portfolio by trading for him through block trading, a form of trading that was exclusively reserved for high net worth clients. Later on in the book, I will examine closely Epstein's oddball relationship with Wexner, including rumors I heard from people in their inner circle that they were gay lovers.

CHAPTER II - IMPORTING
AND EXPORTING

As far as I could research, Epstein started developing his international child sex trafficking ring as far back as the mid-eighties. He recruited most of the underage girls from the streets of Ukraine, France and Brazil. People who worked for him told me he occasionally brought in girls from China and Colombia, a country I'd end up visiting to check a lead I was given about how he ran an elaborate child sex trafficking ring in Medellin, a city renowned for being one of the most dangerous places in the world in the eighties and early nineties when it was ruled by notorious Medellin Cartel narcoterrorist, Pablo Escobar. Through multiple sources once connected to Escobar and Epstein, I learned for several years Epstein had financed an elaborate child sex trafficking ring that would bring girls as young as 11 from Medellin to one of his luxury properties. When I visited Colombia in 2015, I interviewed a former police detective in Medellin who confirmed to me that Epstein's name was on the Colombian authorities radar. "Unfortunately, there's a lot of child sex trafficking in our country," detective Ricardo Garcia told me. "We are well aware that Mr. Epstein was running an international child sex trafficking ring and was recruiting girls from parts of Colombia, including Medellin. He certainly is no friend of ours. In fact I've heard some rumors that Epstein was in touch with Pablo Escobar the last couple years of Escobars' life and was trying to do a deal with Escobar to send young girls to him in Florida in exchange for Epstein arranging Escobar to take asylum in Israel."

According to Garcia, Escobar was keen on escaping Colombia and was looking for the perfect place to start a new life. Israel was on his radar. Epstein, who had been linked in the past to being a secret agent for Israel's national intelligence agency Mossad, promised Escobar that Israel would protect him if he'd invest a few hundred million dollars in its economy. Several people confirmed to me Escobar , a multi billionaire who was listed on Forbes' richest list for seven years, was intrigued by Epstein's offer. A cousin of Escobar said Colombia's most famous drug lord prepared to move to the Holy Land. "Months before Pablo died he started learning Hebrew and reading as much as he could about Israel so he'd be able to assimilate there," the cousin "Jose Vazquez" told me. "He even started observing the Jewish Sabbath, making sure Saturday was a day of rest. He thought Israel would be the best place in the world for him to stay safe."

Later on in the book I will discuss Epstein's ties to Mossad and reveal that he most likely acted as a double agent, also working as a spy for a major Arab country that wanted to destroy Israel. He played both sides like a fiddle.

As far fetched as Escobar and Epstein becoming business partners sounds, I later learned it actually took place. Epstein had no scruples when it came to managing people's money. He'd bend the rules as much as he could to make himself and his clients extra money. Years later, I was introduced to two former high level agents of Israel's notorious security agency, Shin Bet, who would confirm the story.

It happened when I was in Tel Aviv filming a documentary about Pink Floyd leader Roger Waters' antisemitic remarks. Waters called Israel worse than Nazi Germany. Being the son of a Holocaust survivor, I found Waters' remarks extremely false, egregious and anitsemitic. In the film called Wish You Weren't Here, I interviewed everyone from Pope Francis, Tony Blair, Arab leaders to members of the Israeli government. Most people agreed that Waters' call for a boycott of Israel was not the proper gateway to a peaceful, two state solution. Both Jews and Palestinians thought his comparison of Israel to Nazi Germany was outrageous and false. Most agreed that it was fair game to criticize some of Israel's policies but that Waters failed to recognize how Israel was by far the most democratic country in the Middle East, acknowledging women's rights, gay rights and allowing Israeli Arabs to sit in its legislative branch of government, the Knesset.

According to the female operative Shin Bet secret agen, Epstein was already on Israel's radar because he once tried to recruit young girls from Tel Aviv. She told me that she became aware of this after a top security detective in Tel Aviv gave her a lead. It was found out that Epstein hired several scouts to comb the streets of Tel Aviv to recruit young, good looking girls. She also stated something that was completely shocking. According to the information she had received, Epstein and Escobar were trying to set up a child sex trafficking ring together in Israel, one that would see Escobar sending young Colombian girls to Tel Aviv with Epstein's handlers selling them for sex to rich Israeli businessmen. "I got this from a very good source," the agent insisted. "Israel was not one of the major hubs where he recruited girls but he was determined to expand his operation there, all with the help of Pablo Escobar. At one point he started up a small operation in Tel Aviv. It later came up that he was recruiting girls from all over the world. This was back in the early nineties. I learned from one credible source Epstein had also started recruiting girls from Colombia and that he had become close friends with the international drug leader Pablo Escobar."

Several days later I met up with another secret agent source for my Roger Waters documentary who had been high up in Shin Bet during the early nineties. He told me he knew Escobar personally, having sold him two submarines to escape Colombia while he was in hiding from authorities three weeks before he was finally tracked down in Medellin and killed in a shootout with police on a Medellin rooftop. It happened in December 1993. Escobar planned to escape in the submarines to Ecuador where he would have boarded a private jet to fly him to an undisclosed secret location just outside of Israel's border. From there, secret agents would have attempted to get him across the Israeli border with Escobar disguised as a desert dweller Jordanian Bedouin. He would have crossed the border with a fake I.D. card the secret agents arranged for him. The master plan was set to be carried out. According to the undercover agents, the Shin Bet secret operative was dubbed "Operation Pablito".

"Less than a month before Escobar was killed I flew to Medellin to personally meet with Escobar," the former agent revealed. "He was very pro Israel. He asked a lot of questions about how life in Tel Aviv was. He knew a lot about Israel's politics."

I asked the former Shin Bet official if Escobar ended up buying the submarines. "Yes", he replied. "He wanted to use them to escape to a European country and then hop on a plane to Israel. He was a big Zionist and wanted to start a new life in Tel Aviv.

"Escobar turned out to be a man of his word. A couple days after I returned home a man with a suitcase showed up at the front door of my house. He handed it to me. Inside was one hundred and fifty thousand U.S. dollars in cash. That was the price I agreed on with Escobar. Three weeks later he was killed so the deal never went through."

When I asked him what happened to all that cash after Escobar died, he put his index finger over his mouth and said, "That's one thing I can't say. It's secret and too complicated."

Another secret agent who met Escobar six months before he was killed described at length how Escobar was so proud of his connection to Epstein. "He told me he heard the women were stunning in Tel Aviv and in the same sentence he asked me if I knew his friend Jeffrey Epstein," he said. "When I said no, he told me Epstein was a friend of his from New York who was very interested in Israel. He said Epstein convinced him that Israel was rapidly becoming the safest and most prosperous place to live in the world. He seemed very keen to live there."

Although I continued to hear wild stories

about Epstein's recruiting tactics all over the world, the one that stands out most is how he tried to recruit some underage girls from one of the world's most repressive and tyrannical countries - North Korea.

The story goes that Epstein once struck up a conversation with NBA basketball hall-of-famer Dennis Rodman at an exclusive Palm Beach gentlemen's club some fifteen years ago. According to Epstein's employee Pepe, Rodman told Epstein the world would be a safer place if it made peace with the oppressive North Korean regime. Ironically, a few years later Rodman would defy a U.S. government travel warning and fly to North Korea with a group of pro basketball players he assembled to promote sports diplomacy at a time of huge tension between the two countries. It turned out North Korea President Kim Jong-un had been a huge fan of the Chicago Bulls during the nineties, when Rodman won three championships with the team led by Michael Jordan. Although he was vilified by both the media and public for traveling to the isolated Communist country, Rodman eventually would be the person credited with opening the door for peaceful relations between the two countries. Rodman was a contestant on season 8 of Celebrity Apprentice in 2009. It was then that the man nicknamed "The Worm" struck up a friendship with the show's host, future President Donald Trump, despite being fired by Trump for excessive drinking and erratic behavior. Trump brought Rodman back on the show again in 2013 for the show's all star edition. Again Rodman would hear Trump's famous two words after he misspelled the name of America's future first lady on an ad campaign - Melania Trump.

Trump applauded Rodman's efforts to bring the U.S. and North Korea together. In 2013, he said how positive it was that Rodman had become America's "unofficial ambassador" to North Korea. When Trump finally met Kim Jong-un at the historic Singapore Summit in June 2018, Rodman was widely credited for influencing the two leaders to come together.

According to sources who worked for Epstein at his stone mansion with cream-colored walls in Little St. James, Epstein was able to contact Kim Jong-un a year after Rodman's historic visit to Pyongyang and strike a deal with the controversial dictator to allow young North Korean women to fly to his private island. "To this day nobody knows what the exact details of the deal was," said Epstein's former housekeeper Debra Gale. According to multiple sources Kim Jong-un allowed Epstein to send his private luxury Boeing 727 aircraft dubbed "Lolita Express" to Pyongyang to pick up eight beautiful North Korean girls - all virgins. "I wasn't working there then but I've heard from employees that I know well that Mr. Epstein had the girls fly on his private plane and he treated them like princesses."

Epstein's long time right hand man in Paris, Pepe, confirmed the story. He said the two men dubbed it the "Swap Summit". He said "Eppy" bragged about the story for months and told it this way.

"Jeffrey told the North Korean dictator how obsessed he is with Asian women and how he wanted only beautiful young girls. Kim Jong-un was more than willing to oblige, promising Jeffrey every girl on the plane would be gorgeous and would be a virgin. There's many rumors that circulated about what Jeffrey offered in return. People close to him told me he sent a suitcase with three million dollars cash in it, 500 cartons of Camel cigarettes, 400 bottles of different expensive champagnes, and three gorgeous blondes for the dictator to have sex with - two from America and one from Russia; all three lived in St. Martins. I don't think we will ever find out the exact fine print. But a deal was made - I heard Jeffrey brag about it to people in his inner circle. He went on and on about having sex with the North Korean women. He said they were out to please him as much as possible. He claimed to have sex several times a day with all of them. Jeffrey's appetite for sex was insatiable.

"One of his closest household staff members in Little St. James phoned me around that time and told me that he overheard Jeffrey tell his secretary that he had fallen in love with a young girl named Kang Sol-Hye (that's how he recalls hearing Epstein pronounce her name) who was from North Korea. It didn't take long to figure out that girl was one of the girls sent by the North Korean dictator. I remember the other girls who flew on his plane from North Korea went back after a few days. But Sol Hye stayed an extra three weeks. From what I heard, Jeffrey had fallen in love for the first time in years with the young North

Korean beauty. A rumor I heard is that when Epstein finally sent her back home she was killed. Perhaps Kim Jong-un was not happy that she overstayed and made her disappear. That's the only realistic theory I can think of."

Another source who knew Epstein confirmed women from North Korea flew to Pedophile Island but insisted Kim Jong-un was not involved. "Everyone thinks he was involved but I know for a fact he wasn't," the source said. "In fact it was one of his top military aides who did the deal with Epstein behind Kim Jong-un's back. Nobody knows what the exact terms of the deal were but young girls from North Korea were definitely flown to Epstein's island."

One other household employee said Epstein "grossly" overexaggerated what really happened. "It wasn't the first time," the employee said. "He liked to blow things up much bigger than what they really were. I don't believe he did a deal with Kim Jong-un. I know for a fact he didn't. He said that to try to impress people how powerful his connections were. Certainly he loved Asian women. But those girls who showed up were not sent by the North Korean dictator. It's ridiculous if anyone believes it, totally preposterous."

To this day nobody I interviewed was exactly sure where the young, attractive Asian girls came from. "Knowing Jeffrey he said he flew them in from North Korea when in reality he picked them up at some local Chinese restaurant," he said. "Jeffrey liked to blow up everything - from the number of women he slept with to the amount of money in his bank account. Everything with Jeffrey was always inflated."

According to multiple sources, Epstein's private island became dubbed "Pedophile Island" by Epstein's neighbors. Epstein liked to call it "Little St. Jeff's". "Everybody called it 'Pedophile Island,'" Kevin Goodrich, who is from St. Thomas and operates boat charters, said in an interview. "It's our dark corner." Another resident of St. Thomas, Barbara Allen, said she was amazed how the authorities turned a blind eye for so many years to how Epstein imported underage girls to Pedophile Island for sexual activities. "Everyone knew what was going on but it's evident that Epstein paid off key people in order to let him continue bringing in underage girls," she said. "He had a helicopter that would go back and forth to St. Thomas airport with young girls whenever he was in town. He also had a ferry boat that would shuttle dozens of people from St. Thomas who worked for him each day to his island. It was a very well organized process."

CHAPTER III - ROYAL
FASCINATION

There is nothing inherently virtuous about interviewing a sociopath. From the get go, I realized Epstein was nothing more than a narcissistic, sex crazy Wall Street type who believed he was bigger than life. "I can make a woman orgasm by just looking at her," he boasted. "I know how to please a woman better than any other man. That gives me power over them. If you can't dominate a woman you will be run over by her before you can say Yankee Doodle," he claimed. The only connection I had to this maniac was his lifelong obsession with legendary shock jock Howard Stern and The Royal Family. But our views on these subjects differed immensely.

"Howard's god," Epstein said. "He's the only

person in New York who can get more pussy than me. His show is always filled with hot pussy. And he gets millions to smell the girls pussies every day. I would change jobs with him any day. He just sits in his chair in the studio and watches hot pussy come in and out of the studio every day. He has the job every man in the world can only dream of. I don't think he's the most talented host - he certainly is no Johnny Carson or David Letterman. And he's ugly as fuck. He looks like a crossover between Tiny Tim and Weird Al (Yankovic). Howard's living proof that anyone in America, no matter how ugly and infantile they are, can make it. But somehow he turned his shtick into a complete gold mine. Good for him."

Clearly, Epstein was obsessed with Stern. He seemed to know every detail about the private life of the tall, lanky radio host Stern's life. It was Epstein who first alerted me that Stern's constant paranoia and erratic behavior was during the nineties was due to his fear of being rubbed out by the notorious mobsters, the Gambino family, because of his constant derision of legendary crooner, Frank Sinatra. "Frankie put a hit out on Howard," Epstein told me, with a face as serious as a heart attack.

Epstein claimed Stern's constant paranoia completely deflated him. He said the week that the Hollywood movie adaptation of *Private Parts* was released everything came full circle.

"When the movie skyrocketed to number one at the box office during its opening weekend in March 1997, it should have marked the triumphant cap of an extraordinary career, proving that Stern was indeed the King of All Media," Epstein said. "Instead, the occasion was marred by Stern's growing preoccupation with his recent discovery that Frank Sinatra may have ordered a hit on him.

"He was trembling," Epstein continued. "I have a close friend who is close to him. He told me Howard couldn't sleep at night. It drove him to go see a therapist. He thought somebody was going to kill him. It was that bad."

Epstein further explained to me how Stern had recently engaged in an on-air routine — titled "Frank Sinatra Has Alzheimer's — in which he mercilessly and hilariously mocked Sinatra after a report emerged that the aging crooner had been suffering from Alzheimer's-like memory lapses. The piece featured a satirical greatest hits compilation featuring such Sinatra classics as "That's Why The Lady is a Shoe" and "Luck be an Egg Cream Tonight" and invited listeners to order the album by calling the number 1-800-IForgot. On the same show, Stern had also called Sinatra's son Frank Jr. a "loser." This was par for the course for the notorious shock jock and would have normally just been dismissed as his usual schtick. But soon afterwards, Stern heard from a contact that Sinatra was livid and was rumored to have asked his Mafia friends to take "care of that Kike radio prick."

During this period, Stern was a long-time patron of the Manhattan strip club, Scores, rumored to be frequented at the time by notorious members of the Gambino family. He had always been fascinated and intrigued by the club's mob connection, until he learned that he may have been in their cross hairs himself. Famously paranoid and neurotic, the broadcaster became obsessed with the idea that he might end up "wearing cement shoes." This obsession came to a head when Stern learned that a man fitting his own description had been found shot in an alley only blocks from his studio. The man who may or may not have been killed in a case of mistaken identity had the exact same birthday as Stern - January 12. This explained to me why Stern's publisher and close friend once told me, "Howard never goes anywhere without a gun."

In fact, I had my own long-standing connection to Sinatra through my long-time friendship with the singer's ex wife Ava Gardner, who I met during the mid-eighties in London where I spent many evenings at her Hyde Park Towers apartment. Ironically, Gardner revealed to me that she had only moved to England because Sinatra's "people" threatened her. She lived there for decades in fear for her life after she divorced Sinatra in 1957 and refused his repeated entreaties to get back together. She also showed me a scar on her lip from where Sinatra had struck her in a jealous rage. Woody Allen's biographer has revealed that Ol' Blue Eyes had also threatened to have the director "rubbed out" by the Mafia after Sinatra's ex wife Mia Farrow accused Allen of molesting their 7-year-old daughter Dylan. Farrow herself confided that one of her "ex husbands" had offered to break Allen's legs.

Whether or not Sinatra did indeed order a hit on Stern, there is no question that the reclusive broadcaster believed to take the story seriously. Stern's increasing fear sent him on a downward emotional spiral that took a significant toll on his marriage and his career.

"Most scandals usually mean horrible publicity for the person, but Howard keeps things on the down-lo," said Monique Palladino, the founder and head of Radio Gunk, a podcast that dishes the dirt on Stern. "I think he is perceived as a sell-out simply because fans hate how he fawns over people that he once derided and despised, I think Howard was the shy little boy, with very few friends who always sought acceptance, and in this regard, he has always wanted recognition and socialization with those he thinks are "popular" like sitting at the cool kids table at school."

One person close to the famous shock jock elaborated on Monique's claims, saying Stern sold out because he got tired of all the death threats. He said the famous shock jock had to install bullet proof glass at his old CBS studio because he feared someone wanted to shoot him. He stressed, however, that the Sinatra story was only "rumors" that probably was spread to "try to scare Howard".

"I don't believe the Sinatra story at all," he said. "And if they were true Frank wasn't the only dude who wanted to kill Howard. He's received hundreds of death threats." A couple minutes later he backtracked and admitted the Sinatra rumors might have scared the living daylights out of Howard. "But nothing scared him like the Sinatra fiasco. The last thing Howard wanted was to mess with the biggest mobsters in America. He became extremely insecure. He watched every step he took. He thought someone was out to kill him. I had never seen anyone so paranoid."

The *Private Parts* movie famously focused on the remarkable love story between Stern and his college sweetheart Alison Berns — to whom he had always remained faithful despite his infamous public schtick about lusting after beautiful women. Ironically, it was around the time that the movie was released that the couple's storied 21-year-old marriage began to unravel — fueled by Stern's increasing paranoia and erratic behavior which friends and associates linked to the Sinatra rumor. This proved to be the last straw for Alison who separated from her husband before finally filing for divorce in 1999.

"Alison had had enough, she kept getting so humiliated," Epstein told me, while eating a huge pastrami sandwich on black russian bread. It was his second round. Epstein told me he only ate meat occasionally and would be "more than happy" to cheat on his normally healthy diet when he had a chance to eat one of Benash's huge sandwiches. He said he preferred Benash to the famous Carnegie Deli across the street because he found the food to taste "more Jewish, almost as good as mother's home cooking. And, unlike across the street, very few tourists in here," he said.

"Every day Alison had to watch Howard be

around gorgeous models and strippers on his show who would bare all in his studio," Epstein went on. "He was all over them. What woman in their right mind would want to put up with that?"

It was at that time that the legendary shock jock embarked on a raucous journey. a tumultuous two-year period following the divorce in which Stern was finally able to indulge all the raunchy sexcapades and fantasies that he had always titillated his listeners, but from which he had always refrained in real life out of devotion to Alison. I interviewed strippers, models and groupies who Stern allegedly bedded during this period and it paints a colorful and salacious picture of these years — sounding, in fact, much like a typical Stern broadcast. And while the shock jock had always intimated that this experience was his dream come true, I learned something very different and surprising from the man himself. Stern confided that, despite all the beautiful women and casual sex, he was in fact "miserable" during this entire period. He missed Alison and realized too late that he was never cut out to be a "wild man." It was only when he met his future wife, model Beth Ostrosky, that Stern finally came to the realization that he actually preferred monogamy to "a smorgasbord of pussy."

"Howard had access to as much pussy as every man could only dream of," said a former employee at Sirius who once worked with Stern. "But he was never happy. He had all the money in the world to buy anything he wanted at least two times over. But

I always found something very mysterious and dark about him. He lives in his own world. It's extremely disconcerting - frightening."

Many people I interviewed who have followed Stern closely allege the self proclaimed King Of All Media used his fame and fortune to live above the rules applied to everyone else. "All you need to do is listen to the shows we have done pertaining to this, it includes sooooo many clips of his past. He has been very comfortable in the past of using the N word liberally as well as using cultural stereotypes for lazy cheap laughs. Not to mention the wholesale exploitation of mentally challenged people, with zero compensation," the head of Radio Gunk, Monique Palladino said. "Yet the man made millions off them. To this day he has staff members who act like they are friends to these people, all while laughing at them - see Shuli and Underdog Lady."

Another huge critic of the iconic radio host I interviewed was a former colleague of Stern who worked right down the hall from him at Sirius, New York radio legend former co-host of the popular Opie & Anthony show, Anthony Cumia. Cumia, who now owns his own media network called Compound Media, had a lot to say. When I broached the subject of Stern, his face lit up. He didn't have many flattering words.

"I respect what he's accomplished but the man thinks he's larger than life," Cumia told me not long after he left Sirius, sitting backstage eating pizza at his impressive, new Manhattan studio. "He had a car with tinted windows and a driver to Sirius who would go through a secret entrance in the garage in the early hours of the morning. Seriously, as if anyone would be stalking him at that time? When he'd arrive they'd rope off a section to his studio and nobody was allowed to approach him or try to talk to him. It was so ridiculous. I worked at Sirius for many years and never saw him once. He's a man who's obviously extremely paranoid and probably has a lot to hide."

Cumia lambasted Stern, branding him a "complete sellout". "He duped us all," Cumia went on. "He spent all those years bashing all the top celebrities only because he wanted to become one of them himself. He's a complete phony. Now you see him having dinners and going to parties with all these A-listers. That's all he ever wanted, it's quite sad. He should have been upfront with everyone from the beginning that his goal was to become part of the establishment."

Many might jump to the conclusion that Cumia was only spewing sour grapes because he earns barely a fraction of Stern's near annual 100 million dollar salary. Cumia, deeply embroiled in a controversy of his own when he pleaded guilty in 2016 to two misdemeanor charges of allegedly assaulting his then 26-year-old girlfriend Danielle Brand in his Long Island home, insisted the last thing he'd do in life was waste his time being jealous of Stern. "I'm a happy man who enjoys life," Cumia said. "Why in the world would I be jealous of Howard. He leads a miserable, lonely life. Money can't buy you happiness. I'd never change shoes with him, no matter how much money you offered me."

A former Stern show staffer accused the tall, lanky shock jock of being more insecure than "a wife whose husband has cheated on her more than a hundred times with her best friend". "Anyone who gets in his way is a goner," the former staffer said. "Howard's one of the most insecure people one can ever meet. Yes, Anthony Cumia is completely accurate. Howard spent all those years trashing celebs because he was so insecure. He poo-pooed anyone who challenged him. Later on he decided to start becoming more of an interviewer than anything else. And the A-listers bought into it, mainly because of the huge amount of listeners he has every day. They really don't care about Howard, they care about getting publicity to boost their careers. You see him hanging with stars like Jennifer Aniston, Paul McCartney and Jimmy Kimmel. That's not the type of thing that made Howard successful. He made his career making fun of people like that. So, yes he's proven to be somewhat of a hypocrite. You look at a guy like Anthony Cumia's career, he never sold out and he keeps building his unconditional comedic brand of radio talks how with attitude. He's the complete opposite of what Howard turned out to be."

Many people in the media industry I interviewed during my research, however, did have some overwhelming positive things to say about America's most famous radio host. "He's one of a kind," the late legendary New York TV host Joe Franklin once told me. "He makes about a hundred million dollars a year. The money he makes in a year is what you and I make in a morning," Franklin said jokingly. "I remember when Howard first came to New York and was trying to become big. He used to stalk me, run after me when I came out of my office and walked down 8th Avenue. He'd have a demo cassette in his hand and would give it to me and try to get me to put him on my tv show. I only have good things to say about Howard. Who can argue with his success? Like him or hate him, who thought he'd ever succeed in New York, a radio market that eats them up and spits them out in a New York radio second."

A current Sirius XM host, well-known comedian Jim Norton of the Jim & Sam Show, once told me, "Howard certainly has changed over the years but it's hard to argue with his success. He's a living legend."

I've known Judith Regan since 2009. She's one of the people I respect most in the notorious cutthroat New York publishing industry. Judith's a straight talker who always shoots from the hip. What you see is what you get. She's also a decent bowler and avid Karaoke singer, two activities I've had the pleasure of doing with her over the years in Manhattan. Many people credit Judith as being the brainchild behind the huge bestseller, Private Parts. "We spent a lot of time working on the book in my kitchen," Judith told me, who hinted to me she helped Howard craft a lot of the book. "Howard's a total genius. Nobody does it better than him. People don't realize how good an interviewer he is. If he wanted he could work as an interviewer for any show - 60 Minutes, Dateline, all the top shows. And most of all he's an amazing person with a big heart."

When news circulated in Stern's circle that I was writing an expose on him a plethora of former Stern staff members contacted me with damning information. The people I spoke to included his former producer and top radio industry executive Tim Sabean, Stuttering John Melendez and several people who worked on the HS Show for years. What they told me was alarming, enough dirt for a full book which I am currently working on. Tim Sabean told me how Stern mercilessly let him go after he asked for time off when his father was dying of cancer. "It caused me a lot of heartache," he said. "After working on the show for 26 years I was told by Howard that maybe it's time to part ways, all while my father was dying. It completely changed my opinion of Howard forever." Stuttering John shared with me many stories about how insensitive Stern was to his loyal staff of many years. "When Howard found out Artie Lange was being pursued by the Late Late Show to be a host he put a kabbash on the deal right away," Stuttering John said. "It taught me a great lesson because when Jay Leno and The Tonight Show wanted to hire me I kept my lips sealed because I knew Howard would have killed the deal. He didn't want anyone on the show to further their careers. I kept it quiet until the end and it worked because I ended up working in LA with Jay. And let me tell you something, Jay was a class act compared to Howard. Howard's door is always closed and the staff is advised not to talk to him. Jay's door is always open and even the interns can walk in his office and talk to him anytime they want. The atmosphere behind the scenes on Howard's show has been toxic for years. Everybody from Gary to the rest of the staff is not appreciated and underpaid. The highest I ever earned was 85 thousand dollars, and that was only at the end. The show has a 100 million dollar budget. Howard should pay his staff more and appreciated them more. I worked for him for 15 years and was underpaid. Howard wants all the money for himself."

It was at this point of the conversation that Stuttering John almost made me fall off my chair in disgust. He told me how Stern once told him at work to abort his first child because "he said I was unfit to be a father". Stuttering John said he was crushed by Stern's harsh words and lack of sensitivity. When I asked him if Stern is was an emotional terrorist in the workplace he replied without any hesitation. "Yes," he replied. "He doesn't respect anyone except himself. He used everyone on the show for his own benefit and once it served all his purposes he got rid of them. I'm not afraid of him at all and I will speak out to let everyone know what type of tyrant he really was."

I'll get back to Howard later in the book, when I reveal the veracity of a longstanding rumor about him that I was first made aware of by none other than Epstein. Given rise to the bizarre accusations launched by Epstein would be confirmation from one of Stern's closest longtime associates.

When the conversation shifted to the Royal Family, the prolific U.K. institution I have covered for years, Epstein didn't mince words. He started to let loose. It's at that point that I realized Epstein's aura of being loquacious and intelligent was all one big put-on.

"They're geniuses, they're completely brilliant," he said. "They're the richest motherfuckers in this world who essentially are collecting welfare. I'm serious. Everything including the toilet paper they use every day to wipe their asses is paid for by the hard working British taxpayers. They have created a business template that nobody in the world remotely comes close to matching. And they're not to be fucked around with. People end up dead. Look what happened to Diana. She wanted to marry a Muslim and have a baby with him. The Royal Family had her and her boyfriend murdered. I know that for a fact. I know the family personally." I asked Epstein to elaborate on his connection to the Royal Family. At first he was hesitant but after I pressed him some more he started to open up. "Prince Andrew's my closest friend in the world," he said. "I call him Air Miles Andy because of his penchant for traveling. He's a true jet-set. Some of the best times of my life have been in his company. We are very similar. We are both serial sex addicts. He's the only person I have met who is more obsessed with pussy than me. We have shared the same women. From the reports I've got back from them he's the most perverted animal in the bedroom. He likes to engage in stuff that's even kinky to me - and I'm the king of kink!"

When asked what he thought of the Queen, the words Epstein launched were beyond revolting - they were obscene and disgusting.

"My lifelong mission is to (f) her, no matter how old she is," he said with a total straight face. To this day I think he said it half-jokingly, trying to get my attention to make me laugh. I found it far from amusing, especially since I've been a longtime admirer of Her Royal Majesty. More than anything, it was completely outrageous and inappropriate.

"She's certainly not getting it from the Duke of Deception, Prince Philip. He's a total moron who has been with other women and men behind her back for decades. I was told that by people in their inner circle. So before she dies I'd like to give the Queen the greatest night and biggest orgasm of her life. For all she's put up with that bald, crazy, miserable coot the least I can do is give Liz one wild night New York style. She deserves it."

When I asked him if he ever met the Queen he quickly replied, "Yes".

Despite Epstein's demented sexual fantasies about Her Majesty The Queen, after years of exhaust-ive interviews and research into the Epstein case it's time to hold everyone connected to the serial pedophile accountable, starting with the British Royal Family.

The British public do not want to see their Queen merely appear looking majestic on banknotes, they want her to finally step up and give concrete answers about Prince Andrew's true role and connection to the notorious sociopath Epstein. Much of my research focused on the authoritarian methods of the monarchy and how the British Royal Family tried to silence the media and misdirect Andrew's involvement in the global sex abuse scandal. One of the greatest threats to finding out about whether or not Prince Andrew slept with underage women while hanging out with Epstein is that the Royal Family has become so monolithic on this topic, refusing to comment on it properly and launching a concerted campaign to quash all stories in the media. One editor of a leading British newspaper told me in August 2019, "I have my hands tied. Every time I want to publish a story with new information implicating Andrew representative from the Royal Family try to shut it down. They go to great lengths to get any and all stories about Andrew and Epstein stopped. I have never seen them so afraid. It's obvious, if the story about Andrew ever got out properly it could spell the end of the British Monarchy."

But there is something more central to the Royal Family's campaign to control the media. The persona they put on daily is to try to stay calm in a heaving deck, much like they did after Princess Diana's tragic death. But what happens if the veil of secrecy around Andrew's role with Epstein is finally lifted?

"They'd be toast," a former Buckingham Palace employee who worked in media relations told me. "They'd never be able to bounce back from it. They've endured more than their share of scandals over the years but this one would bury them for good. I'm still in contact with many people who work at Buckingham Palace and they refuse to broach the subject of Andrew. It's too sensitive. Nothing good can come from it."

When asked if it's too delicate a subject for present and past employees, the former employee paused before giving a long winded response. "It's not too delicate, it's just the golden rule the Palace has ingrained in their staff - not to utter a word about it, or else! In fact, I have never seen anything like it. The Palace has always had an attitude of no matter what comes their way they can get out of it, regardless of how bad the situation is. They believe after a certain period of time the crisis will dissipate and both the media and public will move on to other topics. In the Prince Andrew underage sex allegations it's one of those situations that will never go away. No matter how hard the Royal Family tries to make it disappear it will always creep back up on them. If the unconditional truth is ever released I think the British public would try to impeach the Royal Family. Because a lot of Andrew's wrongdoings were done on the British taxpayer's tab."

When asked if there was proof that Andrew

was using British taxpayer money to finance his partying endeavors with Epstein the source said "absolutely". He said it was far more "nefarious" than anyone could imagine. I asked him to elaborate and to provide proof.

"I worked for the Royal Family and The Queen was always concerned Andrew would go broke because of his wild spending habits," the source said. "He's always been prone to living a reckless life. He was always jet setting around the world to meet girlfriends, many of them who were known to Buckingham Palace staff. It was no secret that Andrew was the Royal roving playboy. He was infatuated with young, hot women. But I don't think there's any employee past or present that had an idea that he'd be sleeping with underage. After the stories about him sleeping with Virginia Roberts were published I can tell you one thing, the entire Palace was in total shock. There were employees who quit because they were horrified that Roberts said she was trafficked to Prince Andrew while she was an underage teen. A lot of us know his two girls and we were disgusted that their father did something so disgusting and so unethical. The atmosphere at the Palace since the story broke has never been the same. It's been one of total disbelief. Everyone has been walking on eggshells since the story first leaked several years ago." When asked if the there was proof that Prince Andrew slept with underage girls, the employee responded "no".

After an exhausting few years interviewing hundreds of people trying to get to the bottom of whether or not Prince Andrew slept with underage girls, I conclude unwaveringly that there's no conclusive proof. I have yet to see the smoking gun. In fact, one Epstein household employee told me Epstein once had young girls at his home when Prince Andrew was there and tried to fix Andrew up with one of them who didn't look a day over 15. The Prince would have no part of it. "He looked at Epstein and said 'it's not my style, way too young for me Jeffrey'". The employee swears the Prince walked out of the room nodding his head, leaving Epstein alone with the young girls.

Andrew, however, should not be exonerated for his poor judgment for being so closely affiliated with Epstein. Also, it's common knowledge that Epstein procured female company for Andrew. Many witnesses attest to it. But there's no smoking gun proof that any of the females Andrew slept with were underage. Everything he did appeared to be legal, although in very poor taste. Would one top law enforcement official's account to me change my mind? (More on this and the severe allegations against Andrew later in the book).

Buckingham Palace had been trying to inoculate the royals ever since Virginia Roberts Giuffre first made the charges against Andrew public in a 2014 Florida court filing. In the filing, Roberts alleged how she had been trafficked to Andrew at least three times in 2001, when she was only 17 years old. She said she first met Andrew when Epstein and his longtime protege Ghislaine Maxwell took her to the exclusive, members-only Tramp nightclub in Mayfair, one of London's trendiest areas. Giuffre claims it was March 2001 when she was introduced to Britain's notorious Prince.

"I worked at Tramp for about six months during that time and don't remember that night at all," said Alicia Stone, now married and a mother of two who at the time was working as a hostess. "I was young and was impressed by some of the celebrities who'd drop by. Many of the world's biggest stars who were in town would drop by. Most of them were nice. But the one I remember most was Prince Andrew. I had no idea he was such a party animal. He was dancing all night with a girl who looked like she could be his daughter. But it happened during a different night than the one Roberts alleges. I remember that March night well that Giuffre alleges and I don't remember seeing Andrew in the club. When he came in it was impossible for him to go unnoticed. Maybe she got her dates mixed up because I remember Andrew in the club another time with a young woman and they were practically going at it on the dance floor. All this while he was grabbing her tight, pouring his sweat all over her. He was dripping from dancing so much. The club was crowded and steamy. They looked like they needed to get a room. It got a bit out of control."

Years later, Stone would realize who the young girl might have been. "After reading all the stories in the media about her severe allegations it became all too clear. Although I didn't recognize her face in the photo I saw in the newspaper, because she had aged dramatically, it dawned on me that this could have been the girl Andrew was thrusting from behind on the dance floor. But if it was I think she gave the wrong date. Although it was almost a regular thing to see older men with young girls in the club, seeing Andrew dance so close with such a young girl was kind of gross. It was disgusting because I knew he had two daughters and that he was showing poor values. It also hit home to me because my parents got divorced when I was young because my father was caught cheating with a girl 22 years younger than him. Any respect I had for Andrew was gone after that night."

Another source said he was 100 percent certain Maxwell and Epstein took Giuffre to Tramp. His memory, however, was a tad cloudy on the exact date and time it happened. "Maxwell was a regular there," said Andrew Wall, a former Londoner who used to work security at Tramp. "Although I wasn't there that particular night I remember the next shift I overheard a couple of staff members talking about Prince Andrew groping some waif-like teenage girl. Frankly, it was revolting the way they described it. It sounded like they were practically having sex on the dance floor. One of my colleagues told me at one point he saw Andrew biting the poor girl's neck and pulling her hair while they danced together very close. I'm not sure the exact date when it happened.

"Whenever Maxwell came to the club she

was treated like British royalty because she was the wealthy daughter of the late publishing tycoon Robert Maxwell. She was also close friends with the owner Johnny Gold. He made sure Maxwell got preferential treatment when she came because she'd always bring high profile people who would drop loads of money there. She was quite the character. If there's one person I met in this world who thought their shit didn't stink it was her. She thought she was god's gift to the world and would always have her nose in the air as if she owned the place. I couldn't stand her from the first time I met her when she came in with three teenage looking girls who didn't look a day over 15. That first time I met her she brought in two wealthy looking businessmen. It was obvious Maxwell was giving the businessman a great time by having access to the young girls. They plied the girls with shots of tequila and champagne. By the end of the night it was most clear that the businessmen would end up in some hotel room or somewhere having sex with the girls. They acted like pigs all night. They were touching those girls everywhere. I saw it first hand. It was impossible not to notice."

Florida State Court judge Larry Seidlin was the presiding judge in the notorious Anna Nicole Smith case. Seidlin stressed how important it is for Roberts Giuffre to have proof of the exact timeline of events in order to win her case. "If she can prove she was under 18 in statutory rape you don't need consent," Seidlin said. "If she got the timeline wrong and was 18 when she was with Prince Andrew then the whole merits of the case change. She'd have to prove Prince Andrew had sex with her against her will. It's not easy to do. But if she can prove she was 17 at the time it becomes indefensible." (more on the case later in the book).

In a much maligned 2019 interview with BBC presenter Emily Maitlis, the controversial Prince vehemently denied ever being at Tramp with Giuffre. He insisted it could have never taken place on the date Giuffre swore it happened because he was at a Pizza Express in Woking with his then 12-year-old daughter, Princess Beatrice.

"I believe him," said a former friend of the Prince. "He used to go to Pizza Express and other restaurants with his daughters all the time. I'm not saying the Roberts girl is making up the story. But it's possible her memory is not accurate because it was so long ago and she probably erred in her timeline. I don't think Andrew is capable of making up the Pizza Express story. He's not clever enough to come up with a good alibi like that. Lets face it, Andrew has never been the sharpest knife in the drawer. It's not who he is."

Another of the Prince's oldest friends insists the BBC interview was completely premeditated and that Andrew spent hours on end rehearsing the answers to Maitlis' questions. The friend also accused the BBC of staging the entire thing. "They were in contact with Andrew's camp and gave Andrew a heads up on the type of questions they intended to ask him," the friend said. "Andrew had more than enough time to rehearse his answers. But it all back-fired because nobody seemed to believe a word he said. Everybody thought he was lying. If he really wanted this to go away he'd come forward and take a polygraph test.

"Where there's smoke there's certainly fire. I've known Andrew for decades. I love the guy because he's a loyal friend who'd give his friends the shirt off his back when they need help. But let's be clear Andrew's always been a serial womanizer. He's had sex with more girls than Charles, William and Harry put together. And Harry was pretty wild back in the day before he met Meghan. Harry's known to have had dalliances with strippers, models and all types of girls before finally settling down. But Andrew wins the royal gold medal when it comes to womanizing. He's shagged porn stars, actresses, models athletes, politicians and bartenders at clubs. There's even a longstanding rumor that he was having an affair with one of his household staff members when he was still married to Sarah Ferguson, the Duchess of York. It almost ruined his marriage long before him and Fergie separated. Once Fergie got wind of it the household staff member was immediately let go. It wasn't the first time Andrew was accused of cheating on Fergie."

There were many other instances when Fergie accused Andrew of engaging in secret "shagging" behind her back. The marriage seemed destined to be doomed from the stifling hot June summer day they exchanged nuptials at Westminster Abbey in 1986.

Both of their DNA history was extremely promiscuous.

"I don't think there's one person who knew them well that thought the marriage would last," the longtime friend said. " They both had wild sex lives and were not the type to settle down with one person. Looking back I think the entire marriage was a sham. Andrew's main motivation was to appease the Queen. He had already failed in the Queen's eyes because when it came to education he never went beyond high school. Unlike his older brother Charles, who became the first heir to the British throne to receive a university degree. In many people's eyes although Andrew was known to be the Queen's favorite child, he became the biggest failure to the Queen because he was not ambitious and acted disinterested when it came time to studying or better himself. The Queen often thought Andrew's priorities were in the wrong place as she was acutely aware of many of the girls he had on the side. She feared one day it would all come crashing down."

The person the Queen blamed most for Andrew's predicament was none other than herself. For years she feared that Andrew's life would end up in mayhem because of his playboy, jet-set lifestyle. She implored Andrew to change his ways but to no avail. She desperately tried to find a suitable modus vivendi for Andrew to adhere to.

"Andrew was always the Queen's favorite son," a longtime royal insider revealed. "She'd do anything to cover up his screwups, no matter how bad they were. The Queen failed to talk sense into him. She should have exerted more tough love on him in order to avoid having him end up in the deplorable predicament he finds himself in today. I blame the Queen for being too soft on him all these years. He never received the wakeup call he so desperately needed from the Queen. Now the Queen blames herself for how pathetic Andrew has become. She realizes if she would have taken more affirmative action this might have all been avoided."

Wasn't there a lesson to be drawn from Andrew's wild behavior over the years? Many royal insiders I spoke to thought so. Some blame the Queen and Prince Philip for not stopping Andrew decades ago to avoid his wherewithal from ending up so strained. One doesn't have to look further than the long list of undesirable women Andrew dated throughout his adult life to understand how he put the icing on the cake by destroying his life by becoming party pals with the serial child trafficker Epstein. Over the years Andrew dated many gorgeous models and actresses before, during and after his marriage to Sarah Ferguson. He was obsessed with bedding as many beautiful women as he could get. The Queen was not thrilled with his dubious selection of women, including soft porn actress Koo Stark, former playboy model Denise Martell, sexy PR girls Aurelia Cecil and London tv socialite and businesswoman Caroline Stanbury, stunning Philippine model Alexandra Escrat and Croatian swimwear model Monika Jakisik who is 20 years his junior.

The most oddball of his long string of relationships was with none other than grunge star Kurt
Cobain's widow Courtney Love, the wild, outspoken
leader of the Seattle alternative band, Hole. Ironically, I once co-authored a book about Love's involvement in a possible murder conspiracy against Cobain
who at the time of his death was planning to divorce
her. The book, which became a NY Times bestseller,
is called, Love&Death: The Murder of Kurt Cobain.

In 2006, Love claimed that Andrew showed up
at her Hollywood home at one o'clock in the morning
wanting to party with her. 'He's come to Hollywood
to look for chicks," Love told Russell Brand on his talk
show. "I don't know what he expected at my house; I
think he thought it was going to be like a party.'

One former lover of the carousing Prince I
managed to interview revealed Andrew was quite the
gentleman until he convinced her to take a trip with
him to the exotic white-sandy Caribbean island of
Mustique. She claims it happened when he was still
married to The Duchess of York, Sarah Ferguson. "To
this day I feel bad about it because I feel guilty about
ruining his marriage," the former London model said.
When I told her my sources told me Andrew had other
women on the side, she said she still feels guilty to
this day because she helped breakup a marriage." She
claims she met the carousing Prince at a charity func-
tion back in the late eighties.

"The next thing I know he's all over me, wanting my number and making me promise to meet him
somewhere 'very private'," she said. " I was torn be-

cause I knew he was married. But I reluctantly agreed. What young, naive 20-year-old girl wouldn't. I met with him twice at a hotel just outside London where there wasn't a huge risk of being spotted."

She went on to claim they once met for a "romp" at a private villa on the sandy beaches of the stunning island of Mustique "It's there that I realized how sex obsessed Andrew was. He was the baddest boy you could imagine. He made me engage in extreme, kinky sexual activity with him. He had no boundaries. At one point he spanked me like a baby. He told me he had an open marriage arrangement with his wife. At the time I believed him. I was attracted to him but I knew there was no future. After returning to London I never heard from him again. I felt like he used me for a few days so he could live his wildest fantasies. It took me months to get over what happened. Deep down I thought Andrew was a nice man but I was crushed."

The woman, who is now married with one child, insists the alleged tryst was consensual, although "very dirty". "It was completely physical," she said. "I really never got to know him more than that. There were no invitations anywhere, no flowers and certainly no introduction to his family."

Upon reflection, the accuser admitted Prince Andrew did tell her from the beginning that he didn't want anything serious with her. "I must say, as hurt as I was, he was always upfront with me. He told me he was married and never gave me false hopes. It was my fault for falling so hard for him. Even though he was completely honest with me I hoped he would fall in love with me and we would be together forever. I really thought he was the greatest man in the world - the man of my dreams."

A longtime pal of Andrew defended The Prince. "It's easy for a woman to come forward 20 or 30 years after it allegedly happened," the friend said. "It's like the same how Donald Trump was accused of sexual misconduct before the 2016 election. Women come out of the woodwork all the time when it comes to famous people, accusing them of all kinds of nasty things in the bedroom. Often there's truth to these claims, but a lot of the time women do this to make a quick buck. Sure, Andrew is the perfect candidate to be accused of stuff like that. He has a past with dating women who are considered undesirables. But it's important to still give him the benefit of the doubt. He's never gone on trial. We must presume him innocent until proven guilty."

Andrew's Lothario lifestyle would add up to be the most negative frame put on the royal family ever. They have been through a lot of previous scandals, including: less than a year after becoming King in 1936, King Edward VIII renounced the thrown so he could marry Wallis Simpson, an American socialite who had been divorced once and who was going through her second one; Princess Margaret fell in love with a married man and got engaged to him; Squidygate - Princess Diana caught having an affair with James Gilbey who in a transcript of a phone conversation called Diana her by the pet nickname "Squidgy"

53 times; Prince Harry getting photographed in a Nazi costume in 2005 and Sarah Ferguson caught getting her toes licked on vacation with American financial advisor John Bryan while she was still married to Prince Andrew.

Perhaps one some of the biggest revelations I uncovered about the Prince, who was nicknamed Randy Andy long before he married Sarah Ferguson because of his reputation for being a womanizer, would come from the two women connected more closely to Andrew in the past 15 years than anyone else - a stunning supermodel I first met in 2002 who was Andrew's longtime secret girlfriend, and a former female lover and close friend of Andrew's longtime pal Epstein who provided him many opportunities to be around young, willing and gorgeous girls - Ghislaine Maxwell.

CHAPTER IV - LET'S MAKE A DEAL

By 2017, my investigation had progressed substantially, having interviewed numerous key people close to the sociopath Epstein. I had some strong leads. By now it was completely clear to me the man I interviewed some 15 years ago was the ringleader of one of the world's biggest child sex trafficking rings. Through many connections I had made in the Palm Beach community through friends and by playing tennis at various amateur tournaments - I'm an avid club tennis player who served as Chairman of The Board for IATF (The Israeli American Tennis Foundation) from 2018-2020 - I was able to get a better idea of how sleazy Epstein really was. I also got some good background from several law enforcement officials who, along the way, crossed paths with Epstein.

There were, however, many roadblocks that would make my investigation become more complicated. By now, several people in Epstein's camp were now acutely aware I was on his trail and, according to multiple sources, Epstein himself gave orders to his inner circle not to talk to me. Most willingly obliged. He remembered the tell-all expose I did years back on the modeling industry and was intent to shut down my ongoing investigation into his sleazy empire. One close associate of his I contacted told me to "get lost if you know what's good for you". I realized trying to get to the bottom of how Epstein managed to build his enormous wealth and child sex trafficking ring was not the safest way to make a living. I received numerous threats from his legion of loyal bullies who seemed confident they'd have no problem to shut me down. "Whatever you're working on will never see the light of day," one of Epstein's friends in Palm Beach told me. "You're completely wasting your time. There's nothing there. Jeffrey did nothing wrong. You're barking up the wrong tree."

But I was determined not to gloss over how serious Epstein's operation had become just a few years after he was convicted in 2008 by a Florida state court, pleading guilty to procuring an underage girl for prostitution, as well as soliciting a prostitute. His dream team of lawyers back then, led by Alan Dershowitz - the famous former Harvard law school professor who had a reputation for being one of America's top criminal defense lawyers - helped arranged a plea deal that would see the serial pedophile serve only thirteen months, most of it on work release in a private wing of a county jail. As part of the plea deal, Epstein was forced to make payments to victims and register as a sex offender.

Epstein served his sentence at the Palm Beach County Stockade, the sprawling seventeen acres facility located adjacent to the South Florida Fairgrounds. Palm Beach County Stockade is designed exclusively for minimum & medium-security inmates. It holds 967 beds.

"It was more of a country club than anything else," said a prison guard named "Tim" who says he got to meet Epstein there. "From the moment I met him I knew he had a very evil and dark side. Sometimes it's easy for me to tell right away when a new inmate checks in. He was a very complex person who tried to put on a fake persona. It was very easy to see through. I had his number about thirty seconds after meeting him for the first time."

"Tim" pointed out several things about Epstein being at Stockade that according to him "just didn't make any sense at all". He criticized the Palm Beach Police department for placing Epstein at Stockade because it was a place an inmate like Epstein didn't meet the proper criteria. "He should have never been granted permission to be there in the first place," "Tim" pointed out. "Inmates go to Stockade because it helps them reform. The programs they have like drug education, culinary arts and life skills prepare them to go back into the real world once they have served their time. Epstein didn't need these skills and really should have never spent a day there. He should have been in a facility for people who commit high level crimes. Many people I spoke to at Stockade were not pleased that somehow he finagled his way in there. By being there he deprived someone of being there who really could have benefited from the programs offered there."

The aspect of Epstein's sentence that shocked "Tim" most was how easy it was made for Epstein to come and go. "It was like he was checking in and out of an exclusive hotel," he said. "He was allowed to leave and go wherever he pleased for 12 hours a day. It was a complete joke. He was now a registered sex offender but was released on his own recognizance each day. Someone in the police department obviously had his back. The bigger question is who and why?"

Alexander Acosta, who was the U.S Attorney General for the Southern District of Florida, was the prosecutor who negotiated with Dershowitz the highly controversial plea deal that enabled Epstein to avoid a possible life sentence. The deal allowed Epstein to avoid federal prosecution on similar charges. Years later, Acosta would become President Donald Trump's labor secretary from 2017-2019. When Epstein got off his private jet one late Saturday afternoon July 6, 2019 at Teterboro Airport in New Jersey, after landing there from Paris, he was taken into custody, this time by federal agents. Two weeks later Acosta, then under huge pressure from House Democrats and progressive lobbyists, resigned from his duties in the Trump administration.

At a news conference outside the White House attended by President Trump, Acosta admitted the plea deal for Epstein did not go as originally planned. He said it was his intention to have Epstein serve 18 months behind bars, not the paltry 13 months he served while being allowed out during the day on work release. "The work release was complete BS," Acosta told a jam packed White House press corps. "We believe we proceeded appropriately. We did what we did because we wanted to see Epstein go to jail."

Acosta's resignation was not a total surprise. It had only been a few months earlier, February 21, when a federal judge in South Florida ruled that Acosta and the other prosecutors violated the Crime Victims' Rights Act by finalizing Epstein's plea agreement without disclosing it to the alleged victims. Miami Judge Kenneth Marra said prosecutors "misled" the victims to believe that there was still a possibility that Epstein would end being prosecuted in federal court.

It didn't take long for Acosta to lash back at Judge Marra. He pleaded to two separate congressional panels how his hands were tied, stressing how he stepped in to pursue federal charges against Epstein after a Florida grand jury recommended no prison time for state charges. He also described how he diligently worked hard to abort attempts by Epstein's lawyers to get Justice Department officials to tell his team to back off.

"This matter was appealed all the way up to the deputy attorney general's office," Acosta said at a House hearing. "Not because we weren't doing enough but because the contention was that we were too aggressive." Members of the legal community in Florida appeared outraged by Acosta's attempt to do damage control. Many pointed the finger at Acosta, accusing him of engaging in some sort of cover-up.

"It didn't make sense at all," one prominent Palm Beach official said. "America thought they'd seen it all when OJ Simpson got off. But this was equally as gross. There were mountains of documents and tapes proving how Epstein sexually abused underage girls. It wasn't something like the infamous glove incident 'if it doesn't fit you must acquit". The evidence against Epstein was indefensible. He should have gone behind bars for a long time. Something didn't add up in this bizarre plea deal. The entire thing smelled of being one giant cover-up."

One well-known Florida law enforcement official recalled being very incredulous when the plea deal was struck. "Everybody thought they'd put him in prison and throw away the key," said retired Florida Circuit Court judge Larry Seidlin. "He barely spent a day behind bars. Somehow his lawyers were able to save him from spending the rest of his life behind bars. The crimes he committed were not petty crimes, they were extremely serious. To this day people wonder how his lawyers were able to get him off so light. It almost didn't make any sense. The laws in Florida are very strict when it comes to the type of crimes Epstein committed. A lot of people wondered how Epstein was able to get off so light."

According to multiple sources, the sleazy billionaire had the audacity to yell at his legal team after they struck a remarkable deal that essentially got him off the hook. "Epstein was yelling and screaming at Alan (Dershowitz) when he found out he'd have to do time," said Danny Grossman, who used to co-host a weekly internet tv talk show with Dershowitz and is widely known to be one of his closest friends. "His ego was that big. He thought he was above the law and could just pay his way out of jail by paying a fine. Alan's one of the world's top lawyers. He got Epstein the plea deal of the century."

Epstein circumvented the laws of Florida so much that legal experts all over the world were left dumbfounded how he managed to get off so easy.

"One elaborate cover-up," said former Canadian Department of Justice lawyer Patrick Glemaud. "What other explanation could it be? The sentencing in this case stunned people in the legal community all over the world. In any other jurisdiction Epstein would have most likely gone down for life. For some reason in Florida he was able to get off easily. It all didn't make sense considering the nature of the crimes committed. Until the authorities come clean and admit some wrongdoing this case might never be closed, even though Epstein's dead."

Glemaud, who owned the contemporary art gallery in Miami's Design District for three years from 2015-2018, would provide me with key leads on how to get to the bottom of the Epstein file. I attended several high profile art events at his gallery where I ended up meeting a couple of key people connected to the Epstein case. Eventually, they'd help me uncover some never-before-revealed information about Epstein's Florida operation and some explosive details how the Palm Beach authorities might have turned a blind eye to Epstein's crimes because of the "millions" of dollars Epstein donated to the Palm Beach Police Department and others over the years to try to keep people silent about his illegal forays.

"It was a total pay off," one of the sources, a former Palm Beach law enforcement agent, said. "Look at 2004 when Epstein donated almost ninety thousand dollars to the police department, just a few months before they launched the initial police investigation into his crimes. He's not stupid, he knew well in advance they were onto him so he thought he could buy his way out of it. The same day he turned himself in to police was the same day the Palm Beach Police Department issued him back the full amount of money he donated. They had no choice, otherwise it would look like clear payola. But this was not an isolated incident. Epstein tried to pay off everyone who was powerful. He donated millions to Harvard so he could use the powerful network of contacts Harvard had to try to make him look credible and, most of all, to deter law enforcement from coming after him. The man never even went to Harvard, didn't even have any sort of degree. He did the same with Ohio State and Victoria's Secret, both which had ties to his biggest client, multibillionaire Limited Brands owner, Les Wexner. The Miami Herald did a whole investigation into it that disclosed he was donating millions to everyone. while behind their backs he was raping young girls."

The investigation the law enforcement official alluded to was a jaw dropping series of articles exposing how dangerous, sleazy and corrupt Epstein still was, years after his first conviction. The Miami Herald's Perversion of Justice investigative series, spearheaded by award-winning investigative reporter Julie K. Brown, tracked down more than 60 women who claimed to be victims of Epstein's abuse. The well researched series made world headlines, with Brown being widely credited for reopening the Epstein file that seemed to be collecting dust for many years. Her investigation put insurmountable pressure on federal authorities, leading up to Epstein's re-arrest in 2019.

CHAPTER V - FINDING ODESSA

Something told to me by another source in Palm Beach, who I first met playing a pro-am tennis tournament at the luxurious Breakers resort back in 2012, ended up giving me one of my biggest leads. The fifty something tall, well tanned man, said he used to work as a real estate consultant to Epstein. He led me down a path that would take me to the second largest country in Europe on three occasions - Ukraine, a country that was one of Epstein's favorite stomping grounds to recruit beautiful, underage girls. He described to me at length how Epstein mastered the art of using employees to bring local teen girls to his home for sex and paying victims to recruit new victims. Some of the victims he said were as young as 9 years old. And not all of the victims he insisted were girls. "He also liked young boys," he claimed. "He liked to manipulate them and to torture them. He'd sell them for sex. He was a complete neo masochist."

When I pressed him to provide me some proof he told me he had met a girl from Odessa, the third largest city of Ukraine, who would be able to tell me everything. He said the girl had been one of Epstein's main sex slaves for several years starting in the late nineties. "She traveled with him everywhere," he said. "When she started working for Epstein she was barely 16. She witnessed it all. At first he wined and dined her and bought her expensive gifts. It wouldn't be long until he trafficked her out to some of his highest profile clients. I heard rumors she was trafficked out to notable people like President Clinton, a famous soccer player and a former Israeli Prime Minister. I can't prove it 100 percent but I can give you my word. I heard it from very reliable sources in the local community."

My mind started spinning faster and faster. I asked the real estate broker how in the world would I be able to track her down? "Her name is Julia or to pronounce it properly Yulia," he said. "She went back to Odessa many years ago. You'll be able to find her because I know for a fact she now runs her own exclusive escort agency there. She stayed in touch with a couple of local men here who travel to Ukraine for fun once or twice a year. She takes great care of them there, arranging for them to meet young supermodel types who cater to all their sexual desires. I traveled there for the first time about a year ago this time.. I got her contact info from one of the men who I know quite well. When I arrived she arranged for me to have the time of my life. She provided me the opportunity to spend some time with a couple of beautiful local girls. She changes her phone number all the time to avoid getting caught. I'll give you a number I have for her but if she changed it I'll tell you where you'll be able to easily find her. Whatever you do please don't tell her you're a journalist. She gets very paranoid. Tell her you're there on business."

The cell number the real estate broker gave me turned out to be an old number. When I called, some guy who spoke a tad of broken english told me he had the number for more than a year and had no clue who Yulia was. "No such person here," he said in a thick eastern european accent. "This is my number. No Yulia here." It wouldn't take me long to hop on a flight to Ukraine.

A couple days later I got up at dawn, spending a few hours working on a different project I was on deadline for. Later in the day I took a taxi to Miami International Airport to board a flight to Ukraine via Paris. After more than a three hour layover at Charles de Gaulle Airport , my UIA flight (Ukraine International Airlines) finally took off to the country's capital city, Kiev. I stayed in Kiev one night, enjoying a bowl of borscht and a traditional chicken dish at a local restaurant in the heart of a city that was freezing in early March. Nevertheless, I found Kiev to have a lot of charm. With a glass of fine red wine my check came to eleven Ukrainian hryvnia, (the local currency there). It added up to being the equivalent back in 2015 of around four U.S. dollars. The hotel I stayed at was five star rated and cost only forty seven U.S. dollars a night. It had a gym and spa. Quickly, I realized Ukraine was dirt cheap, one of the least expensive countries to travel in all of Europe. The next morning I boarded a flight to Odessa that took just under ninety minutes

Fate, I thought, was mocking me again. I came up with nothing the first two days. I spent hours on end trying to track down Yulia in the stunning city of Odessa on the Black Sea Shore. The Palm Beach realtor had told me it was almost a sure bet I'd find Yulia sipping her coffee most mornings around 11 am at a local antique style coffee shop in the heart of the city called Zheto. I arrived at Zheto the first two mornings around 9am, drinking coffee after coffee while enjoying some amazing carrot cake. Zheto had the ambiance of an old style Parisian cafe. It wasn't difficult to sit there for hours, sip coffee and soak up the inspiring, artistic energy that permeated it's ultra cool interior.

I got there way in advance, in case Yulia arrived early. Although it would be highly unlikely she'd get there before eleven or noon because of the late hours usually associated with running an escort business. I didn't think finding Yulia would be similar to finding a needle in a haystack because of the strong leads I had on her. The description the Palm Beach realtor gave to me was late twenties, medium tall, blonde, always dressed in black, a free hand writing tattoo of the word love on her right arm and a slight scar above her left eye. With a description like that how could I miss?

Nobody I saw the first two mornings coming in and out at Zheto fit her profile. I spent the first night calling every escort agency in Odessa hoping to track her down. But language was a barrier. Everyone who I spoke to barely spoke English and didn't seem to have any idea who Yulia was. The second night I combed every bar in the city center. Still, no Yulia. Finally, things turned around for me on morning three.

A woman fitting Yulia's description entered Zheto around 11:15 am. Immediately, I looked at her wrist to see if she had a tattoo but I couldn't get a close look enough because it was covered by the long black winter coat she had on. She ordered her coffee and proceeded to sit one table away from me. I looked anxiously at her for a couple seconds before working up the courage to break the ice.

"Yulia, is that you Yulia," I said to her. Complete silence is what greeted me. Bingo! Judging by the way she quickly turned her head to glance at me I knew I had the person I was looking for. I started explaining to her how my real estate buddy in Palm Beach told me to contact her while I was visiting Odessa. I told her I was here on business and wanted to have some fun at night. Money, I told her, was no issue.

"Are you a cop?" she asked me. Quickly, I fired

back. "Most certainly not." . Now I was able to see clearly the love tattoo on her wrist because she took off her coat. When I told her the name of our mutual friend who told me to track her down at Zheto, she started laughing. "He's too much," she said. "Telling his friends to stalk me at eleven in the morning. He's such a weird guy. Sweet guy but very weird. Any friend of his is a friend of mine."

Finally, the ice had been broken. She accepted my offer to buy her breakfast. I got right into it, asking her questions pertaining to Palm Beach. She didn't seem to have any filters, going on and on about her many experiences there. She spoke fluent English. "I lived there on- and-off for almost three years," she told me. "But a lot of the time I wasn't there. I was traveling quite a bit." When I asked her what purposes she was traveling for she replied "business, I was in the hospitality business there." I asked Yulia who she worked for in Palm Beach. She replied, "Mr. Jeffrey Epstein, do you know him?" I smiled broadly, replying "Yes, I know him quite well."

"I met him several times some years ago in New York." She asked me what I thought of him. Trying to provoke a strong response out of her I answered, "he seemed quite nice, like the type of guy who speaks the truth, who adheres to a higher set of values than most people."

My response seemed to almost make her fall off her chair. Her soft voice quickly raised several notches. "He's the total opposite," she said. "He convinces everyone he's a saint but in reality he's the biggest sinner one can ever meet."

Miraculously, Yulia started to open up to me about some of the turbulent times she endured being under the powerful spell of Epstein. She described how harmful he was in several insidious ways.

"Everyone falls in love with him at first," she said. "It's so easy to. He can charm the pants off a donkey. I saw so many people fall for it. He basically puts everyone in the clutches of his power by making them intrigued about his wealth and his high profile connections. I got involved with him when I was a few weeks away from turning 16. I was studying ballet in Odessa. Dance is my passion. One day I was approached by a young, good looking guy in the center of Odessa who asked me if I'd be interested in going to London for a long weekend, an all expense paid trip. I thought he was joking but I said "sure". The man told me he worked for one of the world's wealthiest businessmen who was from New York. He promised to take me shopping on the spot if I'd agree to go to London. He told me he'd make all the necessary arrangements for a travel visa and that I'd be treated in London like a "princess".

"For the next two hours he took me to some of Odessa's most expensive stores located on Derybasivska Street." Derybasivska Street is a pedestrian walkway in the center of Odessa that is filled with restaurants and retail stores. "What young girl in Odessa would refuse such an offer?", she said. "Most people can barely afford a loaf of bread there."

The average salary in Ukraine back in 2015 was the equivalent of around two hundred U.S. dollars a month. It was not easy to make ends meet. "I came back here to be with my family and to help them out," Yulia said. "It's sad, but the only way to make good money here is in the escort business. I'm doing it on the side to help finance my school. I'm studying urban planning at the university here."

Yulia went on about the scout for beautiful young girls Epstein sent to Odessa. "He turned out to be really nice, not showing any ulterior motives. He bought me two pairs of expensive high heels, a couple beautiful dresses, two pairs of jeans, some workout clothes and a pair of running shoes. I must admit it felt amazing to be treated so well. I come from a family with nothing. It was the first time in my life I was able to shop without worrying about a price tag."

A few weeks later Yulia said arrangements had been made for her to fly to London for four days. She was picked up at Heathrow Airport by a private driver sent by Epstein's longtime girlfriend, Ghislaine Maxwell. According to Yulia, she was taken to a home in London's exclusive Belgravia area where she was greeted the well-known British socialite Maxwell. It would be Maxwell who initiated Yulia into Epstein's horrifying world of abuse.

"Ghislaine welcomed me with a few gifts when I arrived, including a small coffee table renaissance art book and a cool looking white necklace. The house was immaculate with nice furniture and beautiful paintings. It had a huge artistic vibe. She showed me the way to my room and let me alone to shower. A half hour later I went into the living room. Epstein was there. He welcomed me with a hug and told me to make myself at home. He talked to me at length about dance, he seemed to know a lot about ballet and contemporary dance. Ghislaine opened a bottle of champagne. I remember it distinctly because it was a bottle of Dom Perignon Rose. A couple hours later around 9pm the three of us had finished drinking a second bottle of the Rose champagne. We were beyond tipsy. Ghislaine had some cool chill out music playing in the background on her modern looking sound system. We were all in a good mood. It's around that point when I got my first taste of what life would be like around these two wackjobs."

According to Yulia, Maxwell started dancing close to her and at some point jammed her tongue down her throat. At first, she recalled, squirming a little with guilt and pleasure. "She started touching me and kissing me," Yulia recalled. "I was uncomfortable but by that point I was so drunk that I had completely lost control of myself. Maxwell undid her shirt and put my mouth on her rather large breasts. I started licking them and she started touching me downstairs. To be honest, I don't remember much else except seeing Epstein masturbate next to us while Maxwell was seducing me. They got me so drunk so it's very hard to remember everything. One thing I do remember is that he had a weird shaped penis. It looked deformed. I had never seen anything quite like it. At some point Ghislaine got on her knees and started sucking off Epstein."

Yulia said that first night ended with Maxwell giving her oral sex. She recalled Maxwell throwing herself down on her. "It's the first time anyone ever made me orgasm," Yulia admitted. "She was all over me. I didn't have sex with Epstein that night. The rest of the weekend I had sex with both of them several times a day. They got me addicted. I became their sex toy that weekend. They treated me well, taking me shopping to Harrods and arranging a spa day for me at a local salon. They treated me to a manicure, pedicure and a massage. They got me dolled up, all for their own pleasure. I felt on top of the world because in some twisted way I as if they were my new family. By the end of the weekend they promised to make arrangements to bring me to the U.S. to spend time at Epstein's Palm Beach home. I was all in. Little did I know it would be the worst decision I ever made. If not for them I wouldn't still be doing what I'm doing now. I would be a doctor or some type of professional. I wasted so much time with them and now have to start over, to do things I'm not proud of just to survive. Life here is not easy. Most people here live on the poverty line."

By now, I was convinced Yulia wasn't pulling my leg. The way she described Epstein and Maxwell was congruent with what I heard from other key sources.

Still, Yulia was here to make a sale with me. Before she left she told me she had a beautiful girl for me who would accompany me to dinner that night and do whatever I wanted. She said I'd have to pay two hundred U.S. dollars. I told her I wanted to go out with someone who was smart and that could hold a conversation. I stressed to her how I had no desire to going out with underage girls. She promised me she'd send a woman who was in her early twenties. "Her name is Galyna and she studies architecture and English. She's really smart and very sweet."

Before she left I asked her if she ever met anyone famous during her years with Epstein. "Yes," she replied. "Many famous people came in and out." I asked her to name a few. "I met President Bill Clinton a couple times and I also met Naomi Campbell, who is my favorite model of all time. Both of them were very nice." When I asked her if Clinton ever came on to her, she burst out with in laughter. "Never," she said. "He's so much older than me and such a gentleman. He's one of the smartest people I ever met in my life and he's so present. He treats everyone with amazing respect. I heard rumors about Jeffrey providing girls for him for sex but I never saw any proof. He really is the ultimate gentleman. His energy is so kind and pure. People like to talk and make up rumors. I never saw anything from him that suggested he was with young girls."

When asked if she ever met Prince Andrew, Yulia responded "several times". She claimed that Andrew was one of Epstein's most trusted confidantes. "Jeffrey told Andrew everything about his life - all the good, bad and ugly details," Yulia said. "I always found something to be strange about their relationship which was supposed to be mainly for business purposes. I never had anything with him. I was mainly trafficked out to high end corporate clients who visited Jeffrey for fun and games.

"Jeffrey and Andrew used to spend their time together often in the company of attractive, young girls. On a couple of occasions I saw Andrew disappear for hours with a young redhead who he seemed to be in infatuated with. She couldn't have yet reached her 20th birthday. It was a rule Jeffrey imposed in the house to never ask the guests there any personal questions, especially pertaining to a young girl they went off with for a period of time. It was considered off limits."

When Yulia left the cafe there wasn't much more for me to do that day except to wait for the date she had arranged for me. When Galyna showed up in the lobby of my hotel she was everything and more Yulia had described. It was almost as if the woman of my dreams had shown up. She was tall with long brown hair and the most wide-eyed bright smile I had ever seen. Most of all, she turned out to be a great date. We spent hours talking over a seafood dinner, talking about everything from art to politics to literature. "I read three books a week," she told me. "I love Hemingway. I've read all his books. For Whom The Bell Tolls is my favorite. I've read it four times."

At the end of our four hour dinner I paid Galyna

the two hundred dollar fee I agreed on with Yulia. I must admit I would have liked the night to continue, but deep down I knew it wouldn't be right. The only red glag I had with Galyna was her job on the side entertaining out-of-town guests to make some extra money. Being a longtime germophobe, I didn't think she was the perfect match for me. Otherwise, she seemed to be near perfect. At one point during the night she suggested spending the night with me for "an extra tip". Respectfully, I declined her tempting offer.

I had to stay focused on what I originally traveled here for - to get as much information about Epstein from Yulia. I put Galyna in a taxi and wished her a good night. She seemed a bit confused that I didn't want more. "It was such a nice evening," she said sitting in the back seat of the taxi with the window slightly rolled down. "We will see each other again soon. Please promise me that we will see each other soon."

I told her I had recently got out of a relationship and wanted to take things slow. She said she appreciated how I wasn't in a rush. "One door closes another one opens," she said before her taxi left.

The next day, I met Yulia at the same cafe around 11:30 am. She asked me how my night with Galyna went. I told her, "it was absolutely perfect." She told me she had only a few minutes to talk because she had to run a few errands for her mother, who she said was seriously ill with stage 3 breast cancer. "She's very very ill," Yulia told me. "The doctors aren't sure if she'll make it. It's so sad because she's the closest person in my life. I tell her everything. She knows every detail of all the stuff that happened with Epstein. Her love for me is unconditional. It's the only unconditional love I have ever known."

Before she left, I asked her to describe to me how Epstein was able to run such an elaborate, illegal child sex trafficking ring for so many years. I asked her to describe at length the inner workings of the operation. She gave me explicit details which I'll reveal later in the book.

One thing that stuck with me was Yulia's vivid description about how all her dark premonitions about Maxwell would ring true. "She was hungry for wealth, power and lots of sex," Yulia recounted. "I have never met anyone so obsessed with power. If she felt you were a threat she'd be able to get rid of you in a split second. A close friend of Ghislaine in Paris once warned me to steer clear of her. She told me Ghislaine had the most viscous streak in her temper and that she could do major damage to me. She explained to me how Epstein used to be so obsessed with Princess Diana. It drove Ghislaine bonkers. She got so jealous to the point that according to the friend she phoned Diana six months before her tragic death and threatened her. After that fatal car crash the friend said Epstein confronted Maxwell and asked her if she played any role in Diana's death."

Maxwell became the focus of the Epstein case after Epstein was found hanging in his prison cell in July 2019. The daughter of the late British publishing baron Robert Maxwell, who was noteworthy for being one of the U.K.'s most corrupt businessmen and a suspected spy. Ghislaine moved to the U.S. shortly after her father's death in 1991. Maxwell plunged to his death from his twenty million dollar yacht, Lady Ghislaine, off the Canary Islands, aged 68. Many people close to Maxwell suggested suicide or murder, perhaps by Mossad, the Israeli intelligence service which Maxwell allegedly had longstanding links to.

Maxwell's suspicious death made front page news in the U.K. for weeks. It's initial shock quickly turned to outrage when a near billion U.S. dollars was discovered to be missing from the pension funds in his business empire. Maxwell had illegally diverted the money to use to try to keep afloat his empire which was on the brink of collapse. Headlines such as The Man Who Saved the Mirror would quickly be changed to Maxwell: The Robber.

"Way before Bernie Madoff there was Robert Maxwell," said Department of Justice lawyer Patrick Glemaud. "Maxwell raped the pension fund. So many people lost their livelihood because of his despicable criminal behavior. He only cared about himself and did whatever was necessary to line his own pockets very deep. When he got on his boat I think there was no shortage of people out there who wanted him to fall off the boat because of all the illegal manoeuvres he made to hurt others. To this day, I believe the way he died is highly suspicious."

Former British Ambassador to Washington Peter Jay who was Maxwell's chief of staff from

1986-1989 explained in an interview to the New York Times how Maxwell chose to do business. "He was a peasant to the roots of his fingernails, with the peasant's mistrust of others," Jay said. "Things were run on a need-to-know principle: if you needed to know, you weren't told."

When Ghislaine Maxwell was arrested in Bradford, New Hampshire on July 2, 2020 she was charged with enticement of minors, sex trafficking of children and perjury. During her arrest FBI agents said when they requested to open the door on the stunning property she was living at, Maxwell fled to another room in the large house and closed the door. Assistant U.S. Attorney Alison Moe described how Maxwell posed as a journalist, "Jen Marshall," when she bought the million dollar New Hampshire estate a year before.

"She has the ability to live off the grid indefinitely," Moe said, noting Maxwell's wealth and huge network of international contacts, along with citizenship in the U.S., the United Kingdom and France.

Many were mystified why it took so long for Maxwell to be arrested. To one former friend of Maxwell, the answer appeared to be logical. The enigmatic woman who had been the central target of the FBI investigation since Epstein was found unresponsive in his cell one year before had been planning her escape for many months. Before the feds arrested her, however, they needed to make sure the charges against her would hold up in court.

"They didn't want to end up with egg on their

face. Word on the street was Ghislaine was planning to disappear to some foreign country," the former friend of Maxwell said. "Apparently she told a close friend she needed to leave the U.S. because the heat was on for her. She was well aware that the authorities were on her trail. It would only be a matter of time. One reliable source told me she heard Ghislaine had arranged for a private jet to fly her to France where she would spend a couple of days before flying off to a remote, secret destination where it would be nearly impossible to track her down. In the end The FBI nabbed her before she could make her exit. They won. She stayed in New Hampshire too long. Her time was up."

In the months following Epstein's death, federal agents monitored Maxwell's every move. William F. Sweeney Jr., assistant director in charge of the FBI's New York Field Office, described the operation to nab Maxwell as a group effort involving FBI offices in Boston, New Jersey, Newark, New Haven and Albany.

"We've been discreetly keeping tabs on Maxwell's whereabouts as we worked this investigation," Sweeney explained. "And more recently, we learned she'd slithered away to a gorgeous property in New Hampshire - continuing to live a life of privilege while her victims live with the trauma inflicted upon them years ago."

Maxwell's arrest made me think back to the interview I had with Epstein at Benash back in 2001. At one point, I asked Epstein if he had a regular girlfriend. He told me he did, describing her as the heiress of a wealthy publishing baron. "It's an on-off, love-hate type of relationship," he told me. "After being with her all these years I'm convinced all women are bipolar. Women are crazy. Their emotions run wild."

CHAPTER VI - ACCRETION, DILUTION & SCHMALTZ

For a couple minutes, I watched as Epstein lifted strands of coleslaw from a side plate. His eyes were fiercely concentrated on the job as his fork went deeper and deeper. For over an hour our conversation was framed in a complete comfort zone, talking about life after 911, sports and exchanging corny jokes. Epstein joked about how the deli food we had on our plates was "a heart attack on a plate." He said, "this food is schmaltz. It's the backbone of Yiddish culture. It's a cholesterol extravaganza."

Asking the right questions is an essential part of my job. I tried to take the measure of the man sitting before me, but his tenseness made me slightly uncomfortable. Though poised and controlled, something rumbled just below the surface, ready for a turn toward malevolence. He had the air of a ticking time bomb, which nobody would be able defuse. His big, fat male ego was evidently toxic.

Finally, I summoned the courage to inquire Epstein about what I had come for, asking him questions about allegations of rape and sexual assault in the modeling industry. His response felt like someone putting a knife in my ear.

"That's like asking if the New York Yankees play baseball," Epstein countered. "Of course there is. It's part and parcel of the business. The modeling agents work hard for two benefits - to make money and to fuck the hottest girls in the world. Jean-Luc Brunel is a good friend of mine. He's fucked more underage girls than anybody in the world. That's how he operates. He wines and dines them and promises them fame and fortune with one thing in mind - to get them into his bed. Jean-Luc Brunel is the notorious French model scout who brought underage models to the U.S. on work visas to sex traffic them out to wealthy predators like Epstein. "When I was 13, Brunel brought me to the U.S. from Moscow and lured me into a world of sex, drugs and prostitution," said former Russian model "Natasha". "I was raped and sold to rich men in the industry many times. Brunel told me I'd become a successful mode. Instead I turned out to be a sex slave who was abused for years by his wealthy circle of friends. He ruined both my life and career." (more on Brunel later in the book).

Epstein admitted to me his deep connections in the modeling industry, which back then had a checkered reputation. "I know all the key players in who run the biggest model agencies. They're all in it to fuck as many young girls as they can. If they were in it for other reasons they'd be in other businesses like banking, engineering or medicine. There's no other explanation. And are they wrong? You only live once so why not make the most of it."

After looking down at his half empty plate again, Epstein looked back up at me pitifully. "That's the trouble with young girls," he exclaimed. "They are almost always attractive and willing. They have a daddy type complex. They're girls who fuck you and try to ruin you as soon as you stop giving them sex and money."

I didn't spare a moment of sympathy for Epstein. Now, I realized how sleazy and immoral he really was. He tried to move away from the conversation but I kept focused. "What about yourself?" I asked him. "Do you hang out with underage models? Do you fuck them?"

"Who doesn't," he replied. "Every guy with money and power in New York fucks young, beautiful girls. Its common knowledge."

In spite of the terribly uncomfortable conversation, I was eager to listen to more. I knew very little about Epstein back then, and I hoped that, as a source for my book, he would give me more intricate details. He began chatting away, and as he spoke, I felt more and more uneasy. He was reluctant to elaborate on how young girls were sexually abused in the modeling industry but was not shy to discuss his own interest in pursuing underage girls. By now, I started to get a pretty good sense of the type of sleazebag I was dealing with.

"Sex with underage girls should be decriminalized," he said with a most serious face. "It used to be legal. Many eras in history permitted men to have sex with young girls. There were no laws against it. Look at homosexuality, in most parts of the world it used to be a major crime and in some countries people still receive death sentences for it. I think the world needs to reevaluate how young girls are perceived and how they crave adventure with older men. There should be no limits."

I started to feel a bit panicky. The notorious Wall Street money manager was yielding enormous amounts of information - perhaps too much! I asked Epstein if he'd marry someone underage. The reply I received made me ponder whether or not this man was trying to pull my leg.

"I'm completely against marriage," he replied. "I'm polyamorous. I don't believe in being with one woman. Most marriages end up in divorce. Why in the world would I ever go against the grain? I usually have eight to twelve girlfriends at the same time. And they all know about each other. Often, I sleep with them at the same time. Being with one woman would bore me to tears. I'm living every man's dream. Let's be honest, very few men would pass on the type of lifestyle I've created. Very few women would pass on it too. I'm living everyone's dream, and I live it every day without any guilt or any remorse."

Epstein embodied everything demonic and unspeakable when it came to the subject of the female gender. He bragged to me how he learned how to manipulate young girls mindsets by studying various spiritual practices, including studying with a Peruvian shaman in the Amazon jungle where he learned the psychedelic powers of a traditional Amazonian plant medicine called ayahuasca.

"It was there that I learned how to conquer young girls with spiritual practices," he said. "Several years ago I spent weeks there learning it. I've always been into spirituality and I believe that it makes a person more in tune with their inner self and their true sexual desires. Ever since I practiced with the Shaman I became a completely different person. Any boundaries I had when it came to sex had disappeared. I was enlightened, free spirited and became a sexual god."

One thing that could be fairly said was that Epstein's grandiose narcissism was not short-lived. Although, back in 2001, I readily presumed he was a self-aggrandizing, pathological egomaniac who mainly talked out of his ass, many years later I'd learn his wild ecstasies and gross physical joys unfortunately turned out to be far from some sort of psychological aberration. He was too hard to keep up with, as his mind jumped jumped randomly from one subject to the next.

Shaman Omar, a world renown shaman re-
puted for his profound healing abilities and vast
range of celebrity and high profile clients, spoke to
me on the subject of Epstein's inner battle between
light and dark. He said Epstein's sordid world was
widely frowned upon by credible healers all over the
world.

"These so called "Elite" are referred to as such
because of wealth, fame, power or a combination of
these possessions," he said. "But within this category
of "Elites" you have those whose thirst for power have
no end. These people turn to non-physical sources of
power. What most would refer to as "dark" forces and
entities.

"These djinn, which is the Arabic word for
genie aka demons, would be fed with blood as well as
the energy of fear coupled with the macabre sexual
ceremonies deemed "sex magik" by occultists like
Epstein whose satanic rituals are celebrated as art.

"Jeffrey Epstein, Maxwell and others may have
indeed used these underage teens to exploit the rich
and famous, but their inner circle which includes
the British Prince Andrew, Bill and Hilary Clinton,
Woody Allen and others use these rituals to feed the
demonic entities in which possess them. They trade
their souls for the illusion of power, because as they
obtain power in the form of control over the popu-
lation in this world, they have no control over their
own minds. Like a rabid vampire high, they are no
longer in control of their thirst."

Shaman Omar spoke of how Epstein's "despicable" acts against young girls were "ritualistic torture". "When you look back into history the ruling class always turned to sacrificial rituals using occult practices to lure in these darker forces through offerings of pain and blood, and the people who seek such power are no different," he said. "I have heard from very good sources that Epstein's private island was not the only location. Prince Andrew would host famous and powerful guests at Mustique, the exclusive Caribbean island on which the rich and famous have vacationed for decades. At these private islands they abuse centuries old spiritual practices by scaring and abusing young girls. The most pure energy in the world is purity itself, and that is embodied in each and every soul that materializes into this world. That is why child sacrifices were always the top choice of the ruling class within the world throughout time because it was the sacrifice of this innocence that was the purest nectar to the demonic forces, the genie who grants worldly wishes."

Shaman Omar's assessment of Epstein will strike a chord to many of the legion of young girls who were sexually assaulted by Epstein. Epstein's sex forays, however, were not just relegated to young, innocent girls. One 11-year-old Sri Lankan boy by the name of Yasira described how he was recruited to fly to Epstein's private island in 2014 and turned into a sex slave, only twelve hours after arriving. He said Epstein put him through an intense yoga session, followed by a massage and meditation. Quickly Epstein became a rock star to Yasira. Little did he know, a drink Epstein offered him after the massage session would be laced with ayahuasca.

"It knocked me out," Yasira confided. "The next day he admitted to me he fed me ayahuasca so I could get 'initiated' into his world. I felt like I drifted off the face of the earth. The next thing I know is I woke up in Epstein's bed without any clothes on. He molested me. The next few days he made me perform oral sex on him at least twice a day and made me do extremely perverted sexual acts on him. He even put his pee in a cup and made me drink it. I was so young and scared at the time. I was very scared. He told me if I ever betrayed his trust he would have me put in his helicopter and I'd get thrown out of it thousands of feet in the air to my death. I really had no interest in messing with him. He was a very dangerous person."

Pepe from Toulouse confirmed how Epstein also abused young boys. For the record, there were three people named Pepe affiliated with Epstein, including Epstein's close friend Pepe Fanjul of the billionaire sugar industry family, Pepe Cruz who used to work with Epstein at his ranch in New Mexico and Pepe from Toulouse who became Epstein's right-hand man in recruiting naive, young good-looking people from all over the world.

"Jeffrey definitely was interested in both girls and boys," Pepe confirmed. "Many people don't realize how addicted he was to anybody who was underage. Often, he'd request just young boys for his own pleasure. He'd make them do extremely gross sexual acts. It's hard to believe any person is capable of doing such disgusting things, like shitting on the boys' faces or their chests. He'd poop in a long sock and then smack the boys in the face with it. He'd convince them that his poop was magical powder and that it was an act of spiritual enlightening for them. Pardon the pun, but Jeffrey was so full of shit!"

Yasira said Epstein's disgust reflex was muted, due to him constantly got sexually aroused from faeces. "He was revolting," Yasira said. "He basically arranged for boys like myself to visit his island, so he could molest us or traffic us to some of his rich client friends. And if we didn't abide by what he said he made sure our lives were ruined. There was another young boy there when I was there. He was from Estonia. He was in total shock after Epstein molested him. He wanted to call the police. He was crying hysterically. One of Epstein's body guards offered him a ride by helicopter to the police station in St. Thomas. It was s total set-up. To this day the boy has never been heard from again. I believe that Epstein's bodyguard took the boy in the helicopter and pushed him out thousands of feet in the air in middle of the ocean. I heard from other people Epstein did that to anybody who tried to get in his way. Not only was he a serious sex offender but I truly believe he was also a serial killer."

Yasira's recovery has been remarkable. He said the no-holds barred abuse by Epstein he withstood will never be erased but with the help of counseling and education he was able to move on. At one point he thought moving on would be impossible.

"I had to overcome so much," he said. "But I moved back home and reconnected with family. After I told them what happened they arranged a long healing process for me. Today, I'm enrolled in a business program at university and am very positive about the future. After what happened to me in St. Thomas, no matter what comes my way I'm prepared. Nothing can be worse in life than Epstein."

According to well respected Miami Psychiatrist Dr. Eva Ritvo, the aftermath scars on an underage person who was sexually abused might run too deep to heal.

"Victims of childhood sexual abuse have many multiple psychological sequela including Depression, Anxiety, Post-Traumatic Stress Disorder, Eating Disorders," Dr. Ritvo said. "Substance Use Disorders and more. In extreme cases, victims of childhood sexual abuse may become victims of sex trafficking. It is important to be aware of the frequency of the problem. Mental health professionals and law enforcement must together to prevent childhood sexual abuse and protect our youth. The consequences of childhood sexual abuse are so severe and can be lifelong. In some cases, sequela may be life threatening due to sexually transmitted diseases, depression and other psychiatric issues leading to suicide or death due to overdose."

CHAPTER VII - LADY DI THEORY

As our lunch progressed, Epstein revealed an embarrassment of a more modest nature that was nothing short of hair raising. He described how he stalked several famous women over the years, including Princess Diana. The way he described it with utmost ego-boost seemed shadier than a palm tree. At one point he backtracked, reverting into damage-control mode, but the fallout was already too big to be turned around.

"Princess Diana was a good friend of mine," he began with a most serious face. "In fact it was me who introduced her to Dodi Fayed. If not for me they would have never met. She was the woman of my dreams. I had never been so infatuated with anyone as I was with Lady Di."

When I asked Epstein to elaborate, he tried to bring down the temperature, trying to stay cool and impassive, but he had trouble containing himself.

"I should have never introduced them," he said. "She'd still be alive and those poor boys would have their precious mother in their lives."

Epstein explained to me how he had considerable stakes in Diana and Dodi's relationship working out. "Dodi was a close friend of mine, and I was going to handle their money, to set them up on a path to financial security," he said. "I would have like to be Dodi, I would have given up everything to be with Lady Di but it just wasn't in the cards. I would have been an amazing stepdad to William and Harry. They needed a good father figure in their lives, someone who would make sure their feet were firmly planted on the ground. Prince Charles was not the right person for that role. He was too preoccupied with other things and was somewhat of a flake. He wasn't the male role model the boys so desperately needed."

Dodi was the son of billionaire Mohamed Al-Fayed, on whose yacht Princess Diana holidayed during the summer of 1997 with her two sons. Diana and Dodi had only been romantically linked for a couple of months before the night of August 31 when they sadly died. Before they died Epstein claimed he got a call from Dodi saying they were planning on having a baby and getting married.

"A few days before the car accident Dodi called me and said they were engaged," Epstein claims. "He wasn't one to joke. Dodi's word was his business card. He always kept his word. He also told me they were planning to start a family together and intended to live half the year in New York and the other half in Spain. He asked me to ask my real estate people to start compiling listings of places on the market in Manhattan and assured me they'd come to New York in a couple weeks to buy a place. I had never heard him seem this excited about anything. He told me there would be a wedding in November, very intimate with around 50 close family and friends. Dodi also told me how excited the boys were. He said he got along with them amazing and that Diana wanted him to be a huge presence in their lives."

Epstein then went on about how he believed Mohamed Al-Fayed, father of Dodi, about a massive cover-up in the couple's deaths involving the Royal family, Diana's sister Lady Sarah McCorquodale and the British intelligence services.

"I've been around the Royal Family for years," Epstein said. "They're extremely racist. That's what set the alarms off. The last thing they wanted was for the mother of the future King of England to have a Muslim stepdad. They were livid. And I believe Dodi's father that they were taken out to avoid a major scandal. Anybody who has been close to the Royal Family knows too well that they're most capable of taking out anyone in a London second who poses a threat to them."

Al-Fayed, owner of London's famed Harrods department store, has long claimed that Diana told him that her ex-husband Prince Charles and the queen's husband Prince Philip were intent to "get rid" of her. Almost a decade after the couple's death in February 2008, Fayed told a London High Court inquest how he believed the Royal Family was behind a murder conspiracy. He accused Prince Philip of being a "Nazi" and a "racist". "You want to know his original name - it ends with Frankenstein," Al-Fayed told the court. "Diana suffered for 20 years from this Dracula family...I will not rest until I die. If I lose everything to find the truth."

At the inquest, Al-Fayed confirmed Epstein's story that Diana and Dodi were engaged. Al-Fayed insisted that the couple planned an announcement the Monday after the crash.

Perhaps the biggest revelation Epstein revealed was that Diana had a wooden box with her initials on it that contained all the details about why she feared for her life, Epstein said Dodi told him days before they died that if anything ever happened to them, he needed to make sure someone found the contents in the box. Al-Fayed would mentioned the same wooden box at the the high court inquest.

"Mr. Fayed mentioned the box I remembered how Epstein described it to me," Epstein's close associate Pepe revealed. "Epstein said Dodi seemed worried that someone would try to kill them. I thought he was being a bit paranoid. Unfortunately, he was right. He must have known much more than he was letting on. Dodi must have told him everything."

Al-Fayed claimed after the crash the contents

of the box were stolen so nobody could get to them. At the high court inquest in February 2008, Al-Fayed accused Diana's sister, Lady Sarah McCorquodale, of being complicit in a big cover-up. He said he spoke to her about the wooden box after the crash, but the fact that the contents were later stolen was evidence that she did everything in her power to hide them.

"I think Al-Fayed's argument is valid," a former Palace employee said. "It made perfect sense. Everyone who worked at the Palace in 1997, including myself knew that there would be no happy ending. Prince Philip was furious how Diana went public with her relationship with Dodi Fayed and was intent to do anything in his power to stop it. He didn't want William and Harry to be brought up in a Muslim environment. He thought it would be detrimental to their future and bad publicity for the monarchy."

A former close friend of Diana revealed the wood box theory espoused by Epstein and Al-Fayed has legs to stand on. "Diana feared for her life," the friend who described herself as Diana's "confidante" revealed. "She made it a point to make sure in case anything happened to her that everything was documented. She believed the Royal Family would do everything in their power to destroy her. I had never seen her so happy in her life after she got involved with Dodi. She had been through so much but clearly had a new lease on life. To this day I believe she was killed and I believe members of the Royal Family were involved. It amazes me how she died just a couple of days before she was going to announce to

the world that she had accepted Dodi's marriage pro-
posal. It disgusts me how the Royal Family has been
able to get away with this. One day the truth will
finally be told."

Equally disheartening for Diana's close friend
was this: Epstein claimed Prince Andrew told him
several times how he thought Diana's death was
under mysterious circumstances. Andrew, Epstein
said, believe he was in a binary situation. If he revealed his true thoughts he'd be thrown out of the the
Royal Family forever. If he kept silent he'd have nothing to lose.

"Prince Andrew told me several times how he
believed there was much more Diana's death than
anyone realized," Epstein said during our lengthy
interview. "He had suspicions that his own family
might have had a hand in it. He went on about how
the Queen and Prince Philip disapproved of her new
relationship. He was emphatic how his family would
never murder anyone, but he said he wouldn't put it
past members of his family to get the secret service to
take matters into their own hands. He seemed quite
torn apart by it. I think it drove him to the brink of a
nervous breakdown because he went on and on about
how bad he felt about William and Harry to have be
without their mother. He always credited Diana for
being a role model mum."

Although millions of dollars was spent on
conducting investigations into the couple's fatal accident, numerous police reports, interrogations and
forensic experts have all agreed that Diana had been

in a car driven by a man who was intoxicated. Public pressure forced Met Police to launch Operation Paget, an inquiry to investigate whether there was any truth in the more than 175 different conspiracy theories. The inquiry found none of the theories to have any validity and that the reality was that Diana's death was an unfortunate accident. Still, to this day, conspiracy theories rage. "That's what Epstein said was the cover-up," Claude Pepe said. "To the day he died he was convinced Diana was deliberately killed to spare the Royal Family further embarrassment. He even went as far to accuse them of killing Diana to profit off a life insurance plan so that they princess would be set for life, without having to have a Muslim stepdad which would have created a huge royal scandal."

Pepe said Epstein told him Andrew said the Royal Family carried out a surreptitious vetting process on Dodi Fayed soon after Diana became linked to him. "Jeffrey told me Andrew said the report was not a good one," Pepe said. "There were a lot of secret lovers linked to Dodi and it was found out that he might have had secret children with a young woman in her late teens in the Middle East. The Royal Family became very concerned once they received the report."

As the lunch went on, Epstein moaned the pleasures of overeating. "I eat like this once every two years," he said. "Today's the day. I felt a craving for this type of food."

Epstein claimed his secret friendship with

Diana was longstanding. Although he admitted how she refused his romantic advances, he said she was more than willing to share some of her most intimate secrets with him, including details about her personal life. He described to me how she confirmed to him before Dodi it was a Quebec politician, the same politician who would visit his private island more than a decade later, who really bonded with her better than any man following her divorce to Prince Charles. "Like Dodi, he was also quite the playboy," Epstein said. "He met Diana two years before she died on a trip to London. She fell for him, although at the time she was reluctant to have a long distance type of relationship."

Epstein described the Quebec politician as being ruthless in the political arena but sweet and generous when it came to dealing with women. "He had it all, good looks, money, status and was very worldly," Epstein said. "That's what attracted Diana to him. He combined a charm and intellect that got her very excited. They had a brief affair and from what he told me they were extremely compatible, especially in the bedroom. He told me Diana said it was the best sex she ever had. He said Diana was so turned on that after the first time they had sex she convinced him not to use a condom."

Claude Pepe confirmed the Quebec politician's affair with the famous princess. "It was kept hush hush but the politician leaked it out years later," Pepe said. "I was there one night at the Epstein's island when he described how he they had a huge bond.

He gave very sharp details. There was no chance he made any of it up. He described her body parts and her personality with a lot of details, details that only people who would have met her could have known. He certainly had a way with women. I saw it when he visited the island when all the girls there fell for him in a flash."

A former staff member of the notorious Quebec politician did not deny the link to Diana. "I've heard the rumors many times," the source, who now lives in Florida, confirmed. "I believe it's true because he traveled several times to England for no official reason. It had nothing to do with his job duties. I remember visiting his home when he called in sick a few months after he went to England to pick up some documents, He told me there was an envelope on his desk with the documents. I couldn't help but notice on his bookshelf a framed picture of Diana in regular clothes on the street in London. I really didn't think much of it back then but today it seems to all make sense."

Epstein marveled at how the politician was able to keep it quiet for so many years. "He wanted to avoid getting his name splattered on the front pages of the UK tabloids," Epstein said. "Somehow him and Diana were able to keep it under wraps. It was a secret romance almost out of a spy thriller, exciting and covert."

As the waitress recharged our glasses with more water, Epstein unloaded a huge bombshell. He claimed the politician and Diana had a one night stand with the politicians' mistress who was originally from Jamaica. "I swear on the holiest bible," Epstein said. "I can prove it. Diana was eager to experiment with a woman. They had a threesome one night and apparently it worked out very well. To my knowledge it only happened once."

Whether Epstein was telling the truth is something that might never be known. The sources I spoke to affiliated with Diana or Buckingham Palace had never heard of any such affair. However, they did seem acutely aware of another thing that I'll write about in next week's installment - how Epstein stalked Diana and two other well-known women in the high-profile world linked to royalty. The sociopath was obsessed with these women, instructing members of his security team to stalk them, take secret photographs, and collect as much information on them as they could dig up. According to multiple sources, most of Epstein's stalkers were female. "They differed from their male counterparts," Pepe said. "Jeffrey was nobody's fool. Most people expect stalkers to be male. By having female stalkers, Jeffrey was able to eliminate any possibility of the stalkers getting caught. He was the most conniving person one could ever meet."

CHAPTER VIII -
STALKING ROYALTY

A series of disturbing incidents provides an excellent portrait of how obsessed Epstein was with several celebrities. He harassed several prolific celebrities with harsh methods of intrusive behavior, including spying, unexpectedly confronting them, hacking their email accounts and ordering his employees to follow them. He lived in a fantasy world, often fabricating stories about how he was romantically involved with Princess Diana, Sweden's Princess Madeleine, or France's former first lady Carla Bruni. Why did Epstein invent these false stories? The answer is unfortunately as simple as it seems: it boils down to his gross narcissism and how for most of his adult life he was unable to respect the feelings and boundaries of others.

Several people close to Epstein first noticed his lurch toward stalking when Princess Diana and Prince Charles separated after 11 years of marriage in December 1992. According to multiple sources, Epstein at the time seemed to be on a spectrum between the poles of rational and irrational. What became problematic was how his infatuation with Princess Diana went overboard. Little by little, then more and more and faster and faster Epstein pursued Diana with such shameless vigor that would end up terrifying Britain's beloved Princess.

"He stalked Diana more than anyone else," Claude Pepe revealed. "Never before had Diana been stalked the way Jeffrey did. He had members of his security staff follow her everywhere, taking secret photos of her that they would deliver to Epstein."

Pepe said Epstein collected every little detail about Diana's life, including her size 9 shoe,, her size 8 dress, , her 26-inch waist line and her favorite perfume - Penhaligon's Bluebell. He even knew her favorite snack, McGrady's bread and butter pudding which was a traditional British desert with raisins sprinkled across the top.

"He demanded his staff to give him all the information about Diana and to spare no details," Pepe said. "He believed he would one day replace Prince Charles as the man in her life. He used to send her gifts without a name attached, including a Rolex watch, an expensive pair of Stuart Weitzman heels that cost around $75,000.00, and some expensive art books. He thought she'd be intrigued by having a secret admirer."

Diana was well aware of Epstein's interest in her Because of his close friendship with Prince Andrew, Epstein was able to meet Diana up close several times at Royal functions and once at a charity auction to benefit AIDS research. Andrew made sure Epstein's name was on the guest list.

"He met her and had conversations with her," Claude Pepe revealed. "He used his connections with Prince Andrew to get invited to several events she attended. He even donated money to her most passionate causes. She was very well aware of who he was but for some reason did not show any romantic interest in him. He asked her out numerous times but always got rejected. In fact, one time she just laughed it off telling him after he asked her out for dinner, 'you're so silly'. He had a hard time being rejected by Diana. That's why he accelerated his stalking methods on her. He couldn't take no for an answer."

Princess Diana was very familiar in dealing with stalkers. During her reign she had several, and said in her own words how she had become a prisoner in her own home because of a photographer she accused of stalking her.

"I constantly feel on edge and am unable to go about my daily affairs without feeling anxious and distressed," Diana said in a court affidavit in the nineties used to obtain a restraining order against freelance photographer Martin Stenning.

Diana successfully took on her stalker, winning a restraining order against the obsessed photographer. The High Court granted an order banning Stenning from going within 300 yards of the estranged wife of Prince Charles, heir to the British throne. Diana told the court she had been stalked by Stenning for six to eight months.

Diana described in the affidavit how she encountered "the unavoidability of being continuously followed and photographed as a consequence of my status and duties."

She stressed how Stenning's stalking methods "are calculated to cause me harm," and scared her and threatened her health.

"I have recently had to resort to borrowing other people's cars or crouching on the seat in the back of my chauffeur-driven cars ... I have felt a prisoner in my home," said Diana.

Once she "grabbed his ignition keys, a camera, binoculars, a flash and an invoice book" from Stenning's motorcycle, and returned them through the police.

Stenning's defense was that he was "only doing his job". He was one of dozens of many photographers who hung around Diana's Kensington Palace residence in west London. They often roared off behind Diana's car, following her to Harbor Club, an exclusive gym where she worked out most days and regularly showed up in shorts. They'd also stake out the streets in nearby Knightsbridge, where she'd regularly shop and dine out with friends.

"Diana was stalked not only by Stenning but by dozens of the world's paparazzi for so many years," said Esmond Choueke, a former correspondent for the National Enquirer. "She couldn't go anywhere without being stalked. When Stenning was charged it was no surprise to anyone. It was nothing new. In fact, many people wondered why it took so long."

The Stenning case had actually become something of a cause celebre during the nineties. Many paparazzi renounced their old behaviour and became changed men. Epstein did the total opposite. He decided to take matters into his own hands. He wanted to see just how paranoid Diana was. So, he decided to deploy three members of his staff outside Kensington Palace to carry out round-the-clock surveillance. He implored them to follow Diana, report on who she was with and to photograph her as much as possible. The situation escalated one day when Diana was approached by one of Epstein's men on a London street as she got into her car and was told "Jeffrey Epstein sends regards".

"Clearly Diana was taken aback, a big scared," Claude Pepe said. "She phoned Epstein that same night and told him she thought he was having her followed. He completely denied it. He said if anything when he was in London he'd have members of his team check up on her to protect her, especially in light of what happened with Stenning. He assured her he had her back. Somehow she seemed to buy into it. For years, she was aware how Epstein wanted to pursue her romantically, but she never gave her the time of day. She heard many wild stories of how Epstein, Ghislaine Maxwell and Prince Andrew had wild times together. She wanted no part of that crowd. She was focused on turning her life around after Prince Charles and raising her boys. She kept in contact with Epstein because he was a potential big donor to her many charities and because of his huge connections to wealthy people who were prospective donors. Aside from that she never seemed to give him the time of day."

Diana actually felt kind of bad for Epstein. His attempts to pursue her were a complete, dismal failure. Wherever he pursued her she would let him off with her usual immaculate grace.

"She was never rude to him even though she knew he was probably following her and trying to get her attention all the time," a former Buckingham Palace staff member said. "She didn't think Epstein was a big threat to her. If anything she thought she'd be able to use him as a donor to her many philanthropic forays. A lot of unsolicited gifts used to arrive for Diana at Kensington Palace. In hindsight, it's clear several of them were from Epstein because they were very detailed, only the stuff that insiders would know about Diana like her waist size or wrist size. Obviously, he was obsessed with her and managed to compile every detail of her physical body so he could send her these very precise gifts that very few people other than her immediate family would know how to have her fitted properly for."

When I interviewed Eptein at Benash in 2001,

he made it sound as if him and Diana had some sort of close relationship. "I knew her for many, many years," he told me. "I definitely think she was taken out, murdered! It's so sad, she was sunlight to the world, taken out in the prime of her life. She accomplished so much before leaving us after only 36 years on the planet. Nobody can ever replace her."

Epstein's stalking habits were almost as convoluted as how he recruited underage girls. Having his employees stalk princesses was one of the most effective weapons in his stalking repertoire. No doubt it was the narcissism in him. He made his employees sign non-disclosure agreements that prevented them from outing him for the many indiscretions he carried out.

"That's why it took so many years for things to leak out," Claude Pepe said. "He had everyone's lips sealed for good. Nobody was willing to break their confidentiality agreements because they knew they wouldn't stand a chance to take Jeffrey on. He was too rich and powerful. He'd be able to ruin their lives in a second."

Epstein was weaving a large tapestry for his stalking habits. Many years after Diana's death he set his sights on another high profile princess, this time on the third child of King Carl XVI Gustaf of Sweden. Princess Madeleine had long been a fixture on Stockholm's nightclub scene. The stunning beauty had been dubbed Sweden's wild child. She dated several men in Stockholm before getting engaged to Swedish attorney Jonas Bergstrom in August 2009. In 2010, she called it off after she found out Bergstrom cheated on her during a ski trip. It was the first time in modern history that a royal wedding had been called off because of infidelity.

"She was devastated and embarrassed," a Swedish friend of the couple revealed. "It took her a long time to get over. At first, she started partying and dating other guys to get back at Jonas. Eventually she completely changed her life, marrying a successful American banker and having kids with him. The best thing that ever happened to Madeleine was to get rid of Jonas. That relationship was toxic and was built on lies."

To help Madeleine heal her broken heart she moved to New York City to work for her mother's non-profit World Childhood Foundation, founded by her mother Queen Silvia. It's in New York where Madeleine caught the attention of Epstein. According to multiple sources, Epstein was enamored by the Swedish Princess. He met her at a charity event put on by her mother and became obsessed.

"He once approached me to keep tabs on her," a former employee of World Childhood Foundation revealed. "I knew Epstein from my Wall Street days. I thought he was joking when he made me the offer. I wanted no part of it. But I didn't think he was serious."

According to Claude Pepe, Epstein had his security team follow Madeleine everywhere she went in New York. He even had them follow her back to Stockholm when she took a trip there to visit her family once Christmas. "Nobody had ever seen Jeffrey so obsessed with anyone like that since Princess Diana," he said. "It was frightening. He had people follow her wherever she went. When she went to visit her family in Stockholm. He had people take photos of her smoking cigarettes outside her family home. He knew everything about her."

A former Epstein security guard admitted Epstein had people follow Madeleine around New York. "It became his full-time job," the security guard said. "It was so weird. He had his staff follow her, take pictures of her, especially her feet. He seemed obsessed with getting photos of her feet when she'd go out wearing open toe shoes. He thought her feet were so appealing. He certainly had some sort of foot fetish when it came to the Swedish princess."

The security guard admitted that Epstein had people approach the stunning Swedish princess in the street on several occasions. "They'd go up to her asking for autographs pretending to be fans," he said. "When they went up to her they'd secretly video her so Jeffrey could see the tape and get a better feel of what she was about. He was completely smitten by her. I remember around that time how he imported an underage girl from Europe and changed her name to Madeleine, so he could pretend having sex with the Swedish princess. He was a very sick man, very twisted and extremely wicked."

In New York, Madeleine met the man of her dreams who would change her life forever. British American banker Christopher O'Neill captured her

heart and the radiant lovebirds got engaged in October 2012. According to multiple sources, Epstein was
extremely jealous.

"He did everything he could to try to discredit O'Neill in financial circles," a former Epstein
employee said. "His connections were very deep on
Wall Street. He wanted to ruin the engagement. He
tried to but failed. Epstein felt betrayed because he
lost Diana 15 years before he set his sights on Madeleine. The two women he fell in love with were both
stunning princesses. He failed to get close to either
of them. Despite his huge wealth and power, Epstein
realized that money couldn't buy love. He felt de-
pressed and lost after Madeleine disappeared from his
radar. When she got married a year later in June 2013
he gave up and moved on to other targets. Certainly,
he found it hard to cope with not being able to have a
relationship with a famous princess. He was obsessed
with royalty and had dreams of one day marring a
beautiful princess. It never happened."

The only non princess Epstein stalked was
none other than the self-proclaimed King of All
Media, Howard Stern. Epstein had his security staff
stalk Stern regularly. He said the only man more
powerful with women in New York other than himself was Stern. There's been confirmation how Epstein increased his stalking methods on Stern in the
two-year period following the divorce in which Stern
was finally able to indulge all the raunchy sexcapades and fantasies that he had always titillated his
listeners, but from which he had always refrained in

real life out of devotion to Alison. In fact, Epstein suggested to close friends that he had become friends with Alison in the months leading up the divorce. Epstein told friends how Stern bedded strippers, models and groupies during this period and painted a colorful and salacious picture of these years — sounding, in fact, much like a typical Stern broadcast. "Howard couldn't handle being alone," Epstein told me at Benash. "He could get all the pussy in the world but still he needed someone to trust, someone who would be his friend. I know for a fact he got his rocks off jerking off to porn in his basement. He didn't need anything else to satisfy him. All he needed was someone to be a friend and a mother figure to him. He is a very needy guy."

Epstein talked about the factors that would eventually lead Howard to jump to Sirius XM from terrestrial radio. . Was it really the money that motivated a man who had always cared little about material possessions and who spent most of his time holed up at home watching television in his Manhattan penthouse apartment? Was it, as he claimed, the power to say whatever he wanted to without fear of censorship even though his audience and potential influence was reduced to a fraction of what it had been on terrestrial radio? "No," Epstein insisted. "Howard needs an outlet that would let him say whatever he wants. He's had too many problems with FCC fines and penalties at CBS. He'll eventually jump to an outlet that gives him all the freedom in the world." Perhaps that was the only thing Epstein was right on during our lengthy interview. Howard started broadcasting for Sirius in 2006 in what has generally been described as a "new era of radio".

"When Howard joined Sirius it basically killed talk radio," the late legendary New York broadcasting icon Joe Franklin told me in a 2008 interview. "But it opened the door for everyone to start their own internet broadcasting stations. And it took off big time. If not for Howard I don't think internet radio would have blown up the way it did."

I sat through hours of an interminably ramble by Epstein. A lot of it was about Stern and how he was in awe of the legendary shock jock. Most of it, however, sounded like sheer jealousy. I had no idea what the hell he was talking about when he said him and Prince Andrew used to spend late nights in his living room listening to old episodes of the Stern show. It sounded a bit too far-fetched.

"We'd spend hours listening to old shows," he claimed. "Prince Andrew loved Howard's humor. The only bigger pervert who I ever met other than Howard was Andrew. He was obsessed with pussy. I don't think I can recall having a conversation with Andrew when he didn't go off about hot pussy."

CHAPTER IX - UNSEALED

In late October 2020, Ghislaine Maxwell re-ceived the rude awakening she had tried so hard to avoid. The jailed former partner of Epstein had fought so hard to keep the documents sealed that she argued would tarnish her case with unbearable prejudice. The Miami Herald, whose brilliant expose series in 2018 brought fresh scrutiny to Epstein's crimes, successfully made a case to make the document public and that Maxwell's fear of embarrassment shouldn't stop the public from learning of "the sexual abuse of young girls at the hands of the wealthy and powerful." Hundreds of pages of transcripts were ordered released by U.S. District Judge Loretta A. Preska in a civil lawsuit.

The transcripts revealed how Epstein's ex-girlfriend and pimp denied introducing Britain's Prince Andrew to underage sex partners in a deposition in which she was on the defensive. She called the prince's accuser an "awful fantasist."

"Are we tallying all the lies?" Ghislaine Maxwell demanded during the 2016 deposition, saying she had no recollection of taking Epstein accuser Virginia Giuffre out for a night of clubbing with Andrew in London. "Her tissue of lies is extremely hard to pick apart what is true and what isn't."

"She is an absolute total liar and you all know she lied on multiple things and that is just one other disgusting thing she added," Maxwell insisted, denying having three-way sex with Epstein and Giuffre.

"I never saw any inappropriate underage activities with Jeffrey ever."

For someone exuding such confidence under oath, Maxwell seemed to omit a plethora of other underage accusers who accused her of similar atrocious behavior. One was a former Epstein employee who claims she was recruited by Maxwell at a boutique store on Paris's famous shopping street, Avenue des Champs Elysee. The stunning former model was shopping for a new outfit when Maxwell approached her.

"She came up to me and was so charming," the former model named Adele said. "She just started talking to me and told me she was British and said she lived in Florida. I was 16 at the time. She got me to try on three outfits and offered to pay for them on condition that I meet her and her boyfriend for drinks that night. I was so naive. At first I thought she was so kind. It was one of the biggest mistakes I made in my life."

By the time Adele showed up a few hours later to meet Maxwell and Epstein at Epstein's Paris apartment, Adele claims the couple were tipsy and from the second Adele entered the sprawling apartment the couple couldn't keep their hands off her. Because she's about to join a class action lawsuit, Adele said she could tell me only a few details.

"The gave me champagne from the second I entered," she said. "I remember at one point Maxwell started massaging me and kissing me. I was so helpless because I was drunk. Then, Maxwell started undressing me and forced me into one of the bedrooms. They raped me. I don't remember much but I remember Epstein taking off his clothes and forcing me to have sex while Maxwell held my arms down. Then I remember Maxwell forcing her way onto me and pulling my hair. It's about then I passed out and don't remember another thing except waking up in the bed around 10 the next morning. I was in complete shock. I didn't know what to do."

Adele finished the interview by telling me Epstein hired her as part of his staff as a fashion consultant. "He paid me to be his home shopper," she said. "He told me to go all in. I needed the extra income. That's how he was able to shut me up. Otherwise, I would have reported him to the police."

I asked Adele if she ever had sex with Epstein after that horrific first encounter. "I prefer not saying," she said. "It will come out in court. I am looking for justice and closure. I will say this, while I worked for him he tried to traffick me for sex to numerous high profile people, including two world leaders."

Finally, I asked her if Maxwell was telling the truth, having long insisted she never procured under-age girls for Epstein. "She's lying through her teeth," Adele said. "It's easy to prove she brought Epstein many underage girls to have sex with. I promise you it will be proven in court."

CHAPTER X - DIRTY OLD MEN

Three hours into our lengthy lunch at Benash, I was quite surprised by what Epstein told me about his relationship with his favorite Palm Beach "buddy" - Donald Trump.

"We have shared a very close relationship for many years," Epstein said. "We share a lot of similar interests - business, quality living, traveling and beautiful women. Donald show his incompetence when he puts his foot in his mouth. He likes to be the loudest voice in the room. At least 50 percent of what he spews is usually hot air. That's what makes him so charming to people. He's a huge talker. Big dreams. But he's proven not to be the wisest businessman on the planet. There's many business projects that he's associated himself with over the years that I would have run miles away from. But that's Donald, he learns by his mistakes even though he never admits to making them."

Epstein said he became associated with Trump through mutual Wall Street friends. They maintained a close relationship for more than a decade. "We are very close friends," Epstein revealed. "He's always trying to raise more money from banks for his business ventures and I try to help him out with connections and solid leads."

Based on Epstein's testimony to me regarding Trump, it appears there was nothing more in their relationship than a long friendship. Ever since Epstein died in 2019 the public was led to believe that their relationship went much deeper than just being friends. During my investigation I received many false lead from sources claiming that Trump was involved in Epstein's seedy, dark inner circle connected to his elaborate child trafficking ring. As much as I would have loved to nail America's 45th President, none of the leads remotely panned out.

"Donald liked Jeffrey because of the jet set lifestyle Jeffrey had," said one Palm Beach retired businessman who knew both men very well. "But I don't think Donald was involved in any of the illegal activity Jeffrey engaged in. They were friends on the social circuit, but were not involved in each other's business ventures."

A 2002 New York Magazine profile of Epstein quoted Trump lauding Epstein for his wild side. "I've known Jeff for fifteen years," Trump said. "Terrific guy. He's a lot of fun to be with. It is even said that he likes beautiful women as much as I do, and many of them are on the younger side. No doubt about it - Jeffrey enjoys his social life."

A close longtime associate of Trump insisted Trump in no way was condoning Epstein's notorious playboy lifestyle. "Donald was being honest as he could be," the associate said. "He was drawing attention to Epstein's controversial lifestyle but in no way whatsoever insinuated he was part of it. In fact, he wanted nothing to do with it. He was calling him out. And as time wore on, he distanced himself further from Epstein because Epstein wouldn't change his ways. As much as Donald liked young, beautiful women he had young kids and would never consider being with young girls. It wasn't his style. Sure Donald loves beautiful women but being with young girls like Epstein was around kind of grossed him out."

Sam Nunberg, a former Trump aide, told the Washington Post how Epstein's immense fortune intrigued Trump. "Bottom line," he said, "Donald would hang out with Epstein because he was rich."

Another source I interviewed "Joe", a former Palm Beach resident who claims to have attended at least two of Trump's three marriages, told me he had a "mountain of evidence" linking Trump to Epstein. When I met him in South Beach, Miami I expected him to show up with boxes of files linking

Trump to Epstein. Instead, he showed up with two old photos of Epstein and Trump posing together at social functions. I told him I could not print his wild allegations unless he had some sort of backup. He replied, "it's obvious they were in cahoots. They were close friends. Everybody suspects Jeffrey got Donald involved. I saw them at parties together. Who knows what really went on behind the scenes? But the rumors I've heard clearly imply that Donald was much closer to Epstein than most people realize."

I explained to Joe how I'd be unable to publish his severe allegations unless he provided me with young girls Trump cavorted with or with key witnesses. He replied, "easy, very easy. I'll have that for you in a flash". He never got back to me.

Epstein's personal Rolodex and black book had thousands of contacts listed, including the cell phone numbers of Trump, his wife Melania and a multitude of people closely connected to Trump. Phone records indicated that Trump phoned Epstein on at least two occasions in November 2004. Unsealed flight logs revealed that Trump flew on Epstein's private plane in 1997, one of many trips Trump took on Epstein's planes according to Epstein's brother Mark.

"They were good friends," Mark Epstein told the Washington Post. "I know (Trump) is trying to distance himself, but they were." One of Mark Epstein's closest friends said he thought Trump's relationship with Epstein went much deeper than being just pals.

"Their interests and obsessions were remarkably similar," the friend said. "You'd think that it would be almost impossible for Donald not to be involved in the fun and games Jeffrey indulged in. Mark always seemed to think Donald was more involved than it's ever been disclosed. He once told me Trump loved being around the gorgeous young women Jeffrey usually had around. And he was also struck by Jeffrey's huge wealth.

"I once saw Ghislaine Maxwell talking to Trump at a party. They appeared to be best of friends, rubbing each other on the shoulder and laughing while having a drink."

A close friend of Maxwell corroborated the Trump/Maxwell connection. "I saw them together on at least two occasions," the source said. "They seemed to bond very well. One time Ghislaine bragged to a couple friends how she's slept with Kings, Queen and world leaders. I couldn't help think that the two most obvious choices for world leaders would most likely be Bill Clinton, whom she was close to for many years, and Trump. Whenever it was convenient for her she'd brag about how fond she was of Trump."

During a press briefing at the White House following Maxwell's arrest, Trump was asked by a reporter about the possibility of Maxwell turning powerful men in. Trump shocked the world's media with his response.

"I don't know - I haven't really been following it too much," he responded. "I just wish her well, frankly. I've met her numerous times over the years - especially since I lived in Palm Beach, and I guess they lived in Palm Beach. But I wish her well."

Maxwell's friend said the President's response is extremely concerning. "He basically seemed to be trying to send a message to Ghislaine to keep quiet and somewhere down the line he'd offer her a pardon," she said. "That's the way I took it. It showed that they had somewhat of a long history. Only Ghislaine and Trump know the real truth but I suspect it goes much deeper than just being friends on the social scene. They are two people with huge egos who would match perfectly on any dating app. And both of them have had long histories of being outed as huge sex addicts. From what Ghislaine has hinted over they years, I strongly suspect there's more to their relationship and that if the truth ever came out it would make front page headlines."

Although the friend offered no proof of her suspicions and never openly accused Maxwell and Trump of having a romantic affair, Trump was accused of more severe accusations in the Epstein case. These accusations put huge pressure on him to step down from the 2016 Presidential race. He denied the accusations vehemently and pressed on to victory over Hilary Clinton. During the heat of the race in June 2016, a woman filed a lawsuit in Manhattan claiming that she was raped by Trump and Epstein at a party at Epstein's Manhattan home in 1994. She would have been 13 at the time, when she started out as an aspiring model. Trump and Epstein vigorously denied the woman's charges.

She dropped her lawsuit the week she was supposed to speak out against Trump to the media. One of her lawyer's, Lisa Bloom, alleged her client dropped the suit because of "numerous threats" against her client.

"She has been here all day, ready to do it, but unfortunately she is in terrible fear," Bloom said. Ironically, Bloom's famous attorney mother Gloria Allred was the attorney representing several other women who had accused Trump of sexual assault.

Virginia Roberts Giuffre, who accused Prince Andrew of rape, worked at Trump's Mar-a-Lago club when she was introduced to Epstein, and when she claims Epstein started to traffic her for sex.

"Nobody will ever know if he's innocent or guilty, even if he's forced to take the stand," Maxwell's close friend said. "Anybody who knows Donald Trump knows that getting the truth out of him is more difficult than walking on the moon. He's a compulsive liar. It's been proven time and again, especially during his years as President when the Washington Post revealed he lied to the media and public thousands of times. I challenge him to take a polygraph test. It's the only way we'll ever get to the bottom of his true involvement with Jeffrey."

Udeniably, Trump was one of the first people to set off a plethora of conspiracy theories that Epstein was murdered in a federal jail. He pointed the finger at none other than his biggest political nemesis. Trump was widely accused of perpetrating a right wing conspiracy theory to defame the notorious Clintons.

Hours after Mr. Epstein was found to have supposedly hanged himself in his Manhattan jail cell, Trump retweeted a post from the comedian Terrence Williams linking the Clintons to the death. Mr. Epstein "had information on Bill Clinton & now he's dead," wrote Mr. Williams, a Trump supporter. In an accompanying two-minute video, Mr. Williams remarked that "for some odd reason, people that have information on the Clintons end up dead."

Although there's no proof whatsoever connected to Trump's retweet, his tweet sparked off a huge ongoing debate as to how Epstein really died. Perhaps America's 45th President knew more than he was letting on.

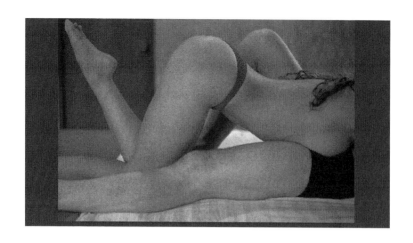

CHAPTER XI - THE BIG SECRET

Sex, it's that simple, and that bedeviling, and that's what it comes down to on Wall Street Epstein told me during the interview at Benash. It's the motivation of every person in the business - the mastery of every money manager and trader whose mastery defies all understanding.

"Everybody on Wall Street is essentially a lost soul," Epstein said. "What they long for is attention, sexual attention. It's the only way they know how to funnel their money for power and dominance over beautiful woman. Anybody who says anything contrary is a total liar."

I asked Epstein if the crave for sexual dominance is

perpetrated more by people in powerful positions like himself. He plowed his fingers through his hair and took pause before finally replying. "Everybody from the top to the lower rung on Wall Street is sex crazed," he replied. Do you realize who you're speaking to? Nobody knows what goes on Wall Street more than me. I've seen guys pay hookers and top models $25,000.00 an hour to please their sexual needs. Some of these power men order male escorts. Wall Street is sex crazed. These powerful men do lots of drugs and pay for sex during their spare time. They don't sit around reading books or watching tv. They're out seven nights a week flashing big money in front of young, naive beautiful people with only one end goal in mind - to get them into their beds by the end of the night. One night they're with a young, gorgeous woman and the next night they're with an impeccably sculpted young male escort. Most people on Wall Street swing every way."

I asked Epstein if he was one of the heavy hitters that swung both ways. Epstein massaged his jaw. "He looked at me straight in the eyes and smiled before flipping open a tiny black book he took out from his jacket pocket. "This is my most important asset," he told me. "Anything I need or want is in here. It's my measuring tool. When I need something I go here. Off the record the answer is a big yes - I, like most people on Wall Street, have certainly indulged on both sides. I'm the most curious person in the world. There's no way I'd go through life with wearing the same color every day. I like variation."

It was at that point that Epstein admitted to me how he was attracted not only to beautiful women but also to beautiful men. He brought up a dalliance he had with a wealthy businessman from my hometown province of Quebec who he remained close to until the last year of his life, according to insiders.

"Jeffrey had a long sexual affair with a wealthy businessman from Montreal," Claude Pepe revealed. "It was no secret how Jeffrey was in love with him for so many years. Even though they kept their affair secret many people close to Jeffrey were aware of what was going on. The businessman who Jeffrey nicknamed "Napoleon" visited his private island many times. They had threesomes and foursomes together, but only with men because Napoleon only like young boys. Whenever they were together they had wild times - lot of alcohol, extravagant parties and orgies every night with young boys. They were completely out of control."

Epstein started talking so openly that I started thinking to myself that, even though the interview was strictly off-the-record, perhaps he was robbing himself of an illusion of safety. Even if I quoted him anonymously in the upcoming models book, back in 2001, certainly many insiders and industry experts would put two and two together. The biggest caveat he revealed was a new slant and perspective on a well-known billionaire who'd turn out to be his biggest client ever - Victoria's Secret chief executive Leslie H. Wexner. Wexner's flagship company Limited Brands had become one of the biggest money making machines in America, largely due to the unparalleled success of his multitude of lingerie retail stores, Victoria's Secret. Wexner was a veritable U.S. multi-billionaire.

"I know Les better than anyone in the world," Epstein told me. "I know everything about his fortune, his eccentric ways and his sex life. He trusts me with everything connected to his life, and he should. I'm the most loyal friend in the world."

Epstein stressed how he hated all the false rumors on Wall Street about his relationship with Wexner, and learned to remove himself from the gruesome details, most of which were couched in the lunchrooms of the high rise towers in downtown Manhattan.

"I don't pay attention to any of it," Epstein said. "I have much more important things to do with my time. Not now or tomorrow, I don't give a fuck what people say. All i care about is that everything I touch brings huge dividends to me and my clients. That's what I get paid to do. This isn't some basketball game in which the score keeps going up and down until the final two minutes. This is life, my life and I have no time to pay attention to nonsense."

Clearly, Epstein started to get defensive about Wexner. But he did reveal one important statement that would serve as a a huge clue years later as to what the extent was of his oddball lengthy relationship with Wexner. "He runs the biggest lingerie company in the world and has the most beautiful models on the planet parading around in Victoria's Secret bras and panties. But, like most other billionaires he certainly has a secret, very secret life. Fitting word for him because he's made most of his fortune off the name secret."

Epstein refused elaborate on what he was implying. "I've given you more than enough on Les," he said. "Lets move on to something else."

Years later when he was arrested a first and then a second time, I was able to piece together what Epstein implied that day. Clearly, he was much closer to Wexner than the world realized.

In the mid eighties, Wexner was introduced to Epstein by a mutual business friend, insurance executive Robert Meister. Meister told Wexner he believed Epstein was one of the most talented "young guns" on Wall Street. He advised Wexner to consider doing business with Epstein. "He's the type of guy who can turn millions into billions," Meister told Wexner. "His financial IQ is one of the highest I've ever come across."

Wexner started spending more time around Epstein, having regular dinner together and even inviting Epstein to spend weekends at his mansion in Columbus, Ohio. "They became almost inseparable," one former Limited Brands executive revealed. "For some reason every financial decision Wexner made went through Epstein. Many of us at Limited Brands were perplexed. We just couldn't understand what was going one. Why would an astute businessman like Wexner entrust his entire fortune to someone like Epstsein, a man who so many people had reservations about. Why would Wexner put all his eggs in one basket?"

Wexner gave Epstein power of attorney over all aspects of his life, including having full authority for him to borrow money on his behalf, to sign his tax returns, to recruit new employees and to make key acquisitions. Furthermore, Wexner took care of Epstein more generously than he did to the closest members of his own family. He turned over a New York mansion which is reputedly one of the the largest apartments ever in New York City, a sprawling estate in Ohio, and a private plane to the hands of Epstein.

"Why the heck did Leslie turn over these gifts valued well over 100 million dollars to his financial advisor," the ex-Limited Brands employee said. "Everyone close to Wexner raised their eyebrows in disbelief. We were all convinced Epstein had some key information on Wexner that Wexner didn't want revealed. It was the only logical explanation."

According to Claude Pepe, Epstein knew the most intimate secrets of Wexner's personal life. "That's why Epstein had a hold on Wexner for so many years," Pepe said. "It had nothing to do with handling his financial portfolio. That was just a way for Wexner to keep Jeffrey busy and on his payroll. It had more to do with how Jeffrey procured sexual favors for Wexner. Wexner was afraid if any of the details were ever released his life would be ruined. He's a man of faith, huge Jewish faith, the last thing he needed was to be outed as a sex crazed old man. That's why he kept Jeffrey working for him for all those years. It was his way of watching over him and keeping him in his clutches."

One brave former Wexner close friend revealed how Epstein and Wexner's relationship went much further than business. "They were family," the former close friend and business associate said. "Epstein had stuff on him that Leslie feared could be used against him. I heard many rumors what went on at the New York apartment. There were also rumblings that Wexner gave Epstein the luxury estate in Ohio, so he could use if for his own secret affairs. Epstein was rarely there. Wexner had the keys and several people I've spoken to believe Epstein procured women and men for Wexner there, so he could sow his sexual seeds."

Perhaps the only way we'll ever know what the true extent of the Epstein and Wexner relationship really was is if Wexner is forced to testify down the line in the string of sex abuse cases that have been launched against the Epstein estate. Still, the rumors of gay sex, orgies and a secret love affair between Epstein and Wexner linger on.

"I know from Wexner's friends that Epstein got male escorts for him," a bestselling author and Vanity Fair contributing writer told me on November 8, 2020. "Epstein basically extorted all his money from Wexner. Wexner was in love with Epstein but there's a debate if Epstein ever was sexual with Wexner."

Another former associate of Wexner who worked for Limited Brands for almost a decade up until 2014 corroborated the Vanity Fair writer's claims. "Male

escorts were ordered regularly," she said. "It's no secret. The only question still out there is if Wexner
was sexually involved with Epstein. He was infatuated with him for years, obsessed with him. He was
the center of his universe. He'd do anything for him.
Most people I've spoken to believes he was deeply in
love with Epstein for years and had trouble letting go,
even when the sex trafficking charges against Epstein
went public. Wexner just couldn't believe Epstein
did anything bad. He was obsessed with him."

Strawberry cheesecake desert arrived more
than five hours after we first started yapping at Benash. Epstein picked up his phone and found Prince
Andrew on the line. They talked for a good 15
minutes, with Epstein laughing almost hysterically
at certain intervals. When the conversation ended
Epstein told me he had sympathy for Andrew. He said
Andrew's ex-wife Sarah Ferguson had been a thorn in
Andrew's side for years, especially when it came to
Andrew trying to move on with new women. The
past few months, Epstein said there had been whis-
pers of Andrew having an affair with leggy redhead
supermodel Angie Everhart. Epstein told me Ferguson called him several times, begging him to do
something about it. He said Ferguson claimed it was
cruel what Andrew was doing to the Royal Family's

reputation.

"She said Andrew had become a huge playboy and the Angie Everhart affair was the final straw," Epstein said. "She told me it's killing her and it's killing the Royal Family. She asked me, being one of Andrew's closest friends, to try to put a stop to it asap."

For years, it was no secret that Andrew was linked to the former Sports Illustrated stunner Everhart. In fact, I met Everhart on at least three occasions during the research process of my models book. One time I met her in my hometown Montreal and twice in Los Angeles, including once at the Standard Hotel when during our conversation she excused herself because Prince Andrew was ringing on her cellphone. Twenty minutes later Everhart returned and practically confessed to me her affair with Andrew.

"He loves redheads," she said. "We are very close. I think he's gorgeous and so charming. He tells me everything. I know pretty much everything that goes on in his life. He trusts me with everything."

A close friend of Prince Andrew confirmed the affair. "They've been shagging for years," Andrew's longtime friend said. "Andrew is obsessed with her. He flies her all over the place for secret trips together and treats her like a princess. They have a wild affair, filled with lots of sex and good times. She's got Andrew wrapped around her little finger like a yo-yo."

Incredibly, it was Feguson who accepted a $19,000 loans from Epstein in 2011 to help pay off a string of huge debts she incurred through lavish spending sprees. She also owed thousand of dollars in backpay to household employees. The infamous redhead Duchess of York was almost a million dollars in debt after her lifestyle company Hartmoor crumbled. According to multiple sources, Queen Elizabeth was reported to be livid and deeply concerned that Ferguson would become the first member of the Royal Family to be declared legally bankrupt. In order to stay afloat, Ferguson took the hefty loan from Epstein to try to stay afloat, a loan she was well aware she was taking from a man who had recently served prison time for committing sex crimes against a minor.

"The Duchess later claimed she regretted taking the money but that was a complete lie," an Epstein associate who used to do financial deals for Prince Andrew named "David" revealed. "She knew what she was doing. She couldn't care less if Epstein was a sex offender or a mass murderer. She has no scruples, and she's shown that time and again in the past. I know for a fact she's slept with wealthy businessmen for financial remuneration. I have met these businessmen. She was basically a Duchess for hire in the bedroom for many years. Everyone in the know were aware if they paid lots of money they'd be able to get her. It made the rounds amongst wealthy businessmen all over the world that the Duchess was for hire. The saying was if you wanted to fuck Fergie you need to show her the money. I know at least two wealthy businessmen who to this day claimed they were successful in bedding her in exchange for 'gifts'. And I'm sure there's many more out there. Today, she seems to have slowed down. But up to a decade ago, she was one of the most sexual redheads in the world for hire. If you had money, Fergie was willing and ready to meet."

Not long after Epstein bailed her out, the disgraced Duchess told The Evening Standard she made a "gigantic error of judgment".

"I abhor pedophilia and any sexual abuse of children," she told the British paper. "I am just so contrite I cannot say. Whenever I can, I will repay the money and will have nothing ever to do with Jeffrey Epstein ever again."

After Epstein caught wind of Ferguson's statements against him he went ballistic. According to multiple sources, Epstein called the Duchess "a pathological liar" and was ready to launch a lawsuit against her. He hired a team of lawyers to force Ferguson into retracting her statements, threatening to sue the pants off her if she didn't comply.

The Duchess's publicist, James Henderson, admitted to CNN that Epstein made a "deeply unpleasant" phone call from Epstein, who didn't mince words. Henderson said Epstein promised to sue Ferguson if she didn't immediately retract her statement of Epstein being a pedophile. Epstein also sent a threatening letter to Ferguson's lawyers in the UK. Epstein's legal counsel at the time was the high priced firm Sitrick & Company, whose founder instructed Epstein to engage a new firm in the UK to take on Ferguson. He hired Paul Tweed, who drafted a statement of retraction that was sent to the Duchess. The statement retracted practically every word of Freguson's initial statement.

The Duchess, fearing her reputation would be ruined forever, refused to play ball with Epstein's lawyers. She refused to retract. Sitrick & Co. sued Epstein in 2014 for more than $71,000 in unpaid legal fees. Ironically, the lawyer Epstein hired in the UK Paul Tweed became close friends with Prince Andrew and Sarah Ferguson, who hired Tweed for other work. Tweed and Andrew became so close, regularly being spotted by the media dining together and playing golf.

"The entire Duchess episode smelled of payoff by the British royals," Claude Pepe said. "I had never seen Jeffrey so upset after the Duchess made those remarks. He swore repeatedly how he'd ruin her for making those statements. He claimed she set him up and played him for a fool. Despite being a convicted sex offender, Jeffrey was a man of power and extreme wealth. He would not be played by anybody as their fool."

When pressed why Epstein was so upset with the Duchess, Pepe revealed the reason why. "Jeffrey told me partied with the Duchess and slept with her on several occasions," Pepe revealed. "That's why I believe he went ballistic after she referred to him as being a pedophile. He just couldn't accept her hypocrisy. He felt she used him in every way possible. He couldn't accept her shifting the blame on him and playing like she was some innocent victim. One thing is super clear - the Duchess knew she was dealing and playing around with a convicted sex offender. She had no shame. She wanted a piece of Jeffrey's fortune and would do anything she had to do to get a piece of it."

Another person in Epstein's inner circle corroborated Pepe's claims. "Sarah Ferguson was a woman for hire," Epstein's former employee and confidante "Mary" said. "She was after Jeffrey for his money. In fact, she'd call him repeatedly and sweet talk him. I once overheard one of their conversations because Jeffrey had her on speaker phone. It sounded like she was trying to have phone sex with him, calling him 'baby' and 'sweetie' and telling him she'd do anything he wanted her to do. She also called him 'handsome' and 'sexy'. So when she turned around and tried to throw him under the bus in the media, Jeffrey felt he had to stand up for himself because she was no angel. In fact, Jeffrey told me the Duchess was the biggest 'devil' he ever met, and he met many during his time. I'll never forget how he told me around the time she accused him in the media that the Duchess was like a 'hooker in heat who would rob their own mother for ten cents."

According to multiple sources, Epstein saw a greater imperative with his close relationship with Prince Andrew. He sold Prince Andrew's most intimate secrets to several notorious foreign intelligence agencies, including Israel's Mossad, the kingdom of Saudi Arabia and the Mukhabarat el-Jamahiriya which was the national intelligence service of Libya under the rule of Muammar Gaddafi. Epstein duped everyone, becoming one of the first people in modern history to be up to his eyeballs in the granular espionage for three powerful regimes.

"Rumors were rife for a long time that Jeffrey was a spy for the Israelis," Claude Pepe revealed. "But later it came out that he was also involved in covert operations for the Saudis and for Libya. Incredibly, he got away with it and details only started leaking after his death. I wouldn't be surprised if there's more countries he shared secret intelligence with. He had this private room that was always locked up. It had lots of computer equipment, including six screens, microphones, dozens of hard drives and extremely protected codes and passwords. Nobody was allowed to enter that room ever. If you were caught near it Jeffrey would fire you. That's where all his covert work for foreign countries took place."

According to multiple sources, Epstein sold a lot of secret information about Prince Andrew to the Israeli Mossad, including videos and recordings. One former Epstein employee described how Epstein installed honeypot cameras on all his properties, so he'd be able to sell the recordings to the Israelis. Epstein also blackmailed the famous people who visited his homes.

"He taped everyone who entered getting massages, having sex, orgies or paying him for services," the former Epstein employee said. "He thought the only way to have the upper hand on these powerful people was to have them on tape. Many of the people recorded, including Prince Andrew, Leslie Wexner and Bill Clinton ended up on their knees, begging Epstein to delete the tapes. They feared their lives would be ruined if the tapes were ever released."

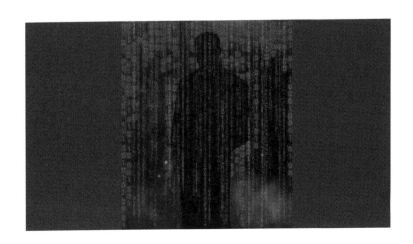

CHAPTER XII - SAUDI/ISRAEL/
LIBYA "TRIPLE AGENT"

During the course of the filming for the documentary I directed about contemporary antisemitism, Wish You Were Weren't Here, I met one former Mossad agent who told me had explosive information about Epstein's ties to Israel. After pressing him for more info when we met at Jeremiah Cafe in Tel Aviv, he started to spill the beans.

"There's no doubt Epstein was involved with Israel's secret service for a long time," he said. "Ghislaine Maxwell's later father Robert Maxwell used to pour millions into the Massad. Ghislaine was the person who introduced Epstein to prominent secret service figures in Israel. Epstein raised them a lot of money through his pro Israel Wall Street contacts in the U.S. But later he found a clever way to profit shamelessly, by selling the secret sex tapes of prominent people like Prince Andrew to Israeli Intelligence services. Apparently the tapes are extremely revealing. If they ever get leaked I think it would spell the end of the British Royal Family.

"The reason why Mossad wanted the tapes so badly was to essentially send a strong message to the Royal Family that if contemporary antisemitism continues to rise in the UK that they would reveal the incriminating tapes that would destroy the royal family forever. Antisemitism in the UK had by far the most documented incidents in the western world, far ahead of the U.S., Germany and France. Our covert investigation revealed the Muslim Brotherhood had secret bunkers all over the UK and were preparing to attack all Jews living in the UK. They spent millions on this terrorist operation. By having the tapes of Andrew it was a powerful way of letting the Royal Family and the British government know that these attacks would not be tolerated and if they continued the sought after videos of Prince Andrew would be released."

The former secret agent said Epstein's master plan was a monster, huge scale plan to take down the world's powerful elite. The secret tapes, he said, is the primary reason why it has taken so long for the authorities to comment on their existence.

"When Epstein died the FBI was able to seize a lot of the tapes that were left on his properties," he said. "But most of the tapes they were looking for were missing. They still have not been able to track them down. Little do they know most of those key, incriminating tapes are in the hands of the Israelis and the Saudis. Epstein sold them to their secret service for major dollars. Epstein was known to be able to turn anything into profit. From what I've heard, he made millions selling those secret tapes. Somewhere down the road those tapes will be leaked, but it won't be by the FBI because they don't have them."

Epstein's ties to the Saudis are even more mind-blowing. Epstein claimed he had been close for years to the Crown Prince Mohammed bin Salman bin Adbulaziz. After Epstein died, police raided his Manhattan mansion and found he had a valid Austrian passport with a fake name, a Saudi residence and his photograph. Also discovered was a framed picture of Mohammed bin Salman in his sprawling New York residence and proof Epstein had made several trips to Saudi to meet with his close royal friend. Epstein's close relationship to the Saudis spanned generations. He started visiting the wealthy Arabian Peninsula as far back as the early eighties, when he invested in several prosperous oil deals there. Amongst the Saudi contacts discovered in Epstein's black book, stolen by his butler and then seized by the FBI, was Prince Salman and the ruling Saud monarchy. Aside from bin Salman, other Saudi contact numbers included King Salman, the country's longtime envoy to Washington Prince Bandar, Saudi businessman Amr Dabbagh and Saudi-Syrian businessman Wafic Said. Sources in Epstein's coterie of associates and friends maintain that Epstein was the closest Jew in the world to the Saudis and had done billions of dollars of deals with them for close to four decades.

"He was one of the closest people in the western world to the Saudi Crown Prince," Claude Pepe said. "They spoke regularly. They had were involved in projects together, to what extent I don't anyone will ever know. But they certainly were much closer than most people realize. One of Epstein's friends told me Epstein gave bin Salman very detailed information about the Israelis. That's how he operated. Jeffrey was the biggest shark of them all, he played all sides for profit."

Another source close to Epstein said the oddball relationship went far beyond security and stocks. He claimed Epstein had a mistress in Riyadh, the capital city of Saudi Arabia, arranged by none other than bin Salman.

"It happened after he went to prison," the close Epstein source revealed. "Epstein and bin Salman started doing business. They became good friends. On one of his trips to Riyadh Epstein fell in love with a stunning 19-year-old engineering student introduced to him by the Crown Prince. Epstein was enamored with her, showering her and her family with expensive gifts and even buying them a luxurious property in the heart of the city. She taught him all about Saudi history and culture. I believe the affair lasted until the day Jeffrey died. Prior to his second arrest Jeffrey told me on several occasions he was planning to migrate to Saudi Arabia full time. He was tired of the west and felt the new land of opportunity was in the world's oil capital. He started making plans. For the first time I think Jeffrey found the woman of his dreams and was finally ready to settle down. I know for a fact he started shopping for rings. I truly believe he was planning to marry the young Saudi woman."

One person inextricably linked to Epstein's Saudi connection was the world's richest man, Amazon CEO Jeff Bezos. Bezos and Epstein crossed paths on several occasions, including two "billionaires dinners" in 2004 and 2011 hosted by the Edge Foundation. In fact, the wealthy U.S. moguls happened to be in Riyadh at the same time in November 2016. Was it a strange coincidence?

The Saudi Crown Prince claimed the meetings were unrelated, and that Bezos was there to discuss future investment opportunities. The Saudi Press Agency described Bezos' meeting in a statement: "They discussed fields of cooperation and investment opportunities available according to the Kingdom's Vision 2030."

Some people close to Epstein to this day remain unconvinced. One of Epstein's associates accused the Saudi Crown Prince was trying to cover things up. He said, although Bezos was unaware at the time of Epstein's deep ties to Saudi Arabia, the Crown Prince was trying to get Bezos in his inner circle at Epstein's behest.

"Epstein told bin Salman that within a few years Bezos would be the world's most powerful man," the source said. "He advised him to do any-thing and everything to get as close to Bezos as he possibly could. He also strongly advised him to try to seal a deal with Bezos to invest in Saudi Arabia. Epstein told bin Salman that Bezos would be more rich and powerful than Bill Gates and Warren Buffett within two years. Jeffrey was spot on. As bad a per-son as he was, Jeffrey was a master businessman and a master financial forecaster. Nobody in the world could predict the financial future better than Jeffrey Epstein."

Among powerful world arms dealers and money launder lords, Epstein and bin Salman were re-nowned. They were known as business savants with close ties to the world's richest and elite businessmen in the Middle East and Asia. Moreover, their huge egos and reputations to resort to dirty deeds, including blackmail, to close a business deal was as wide and verdant as a Saudi oil field. In early 2019, Jeff Bezos' chief of security accused the Saudi monarchy of hack-ing into Bezos' personal files, gaining illegal access to his personal messages and explicit, intimate photos. The Daily Beast reported the Saudis' master plan was to blackmail Bezos, who bought The Washington Post in 2013, as retribution for his paper's accusatory coverage of the death of their own columnist, Jamal Khashoggi, whom secret service Saudi agents assas-sinated in Istanbul on October 2, 2018.

To this day, the Saudis vehemently deny the allegations of blackmail against Bezos. Many people blamed the brother of Bezos' mistress Lauren Sanchez, the stunning Emmy Award-winning news anchor, for throwing Bezos under the bus. Michael Sanchez admitted he made a "deal with the devil", selling the story of his sister's affair to the National Enquirer for $200,00. Sanchez strongly denied obtaining the photos, including selfies of Bezos' genitalia. In an interview with the NY Post Page 6, Sanchez said: "I may have helped the Enquirer with their story, but I never had access to the penis selfies."

A top former Epstein associate claims that Epstein was responsible for orchestrating the entire blackmail operation against Bezos. "Coincidences add up," he said. "Epstein and Bezos' private planes were in Riyadh the same day. Epstein, for many years, fuelled the Saudis with secret information about Bezos. Clearly, they were out to blackmail Bezos. And only one person in the world was capable of orchestrating it - Jeffrey Epstein. The photographs with Bezos' private parts exposed and the text messages had Epstein written all over it. That's how he operated. He had similar files on all the people he stalked over the years, including Princess Diana, Princess Madeleine, Prince Andrew, Howard Stern and many others. He was a scumbag to resort to such low class maneuvers but it's the only way he believed he'd be able to always have the upper hand on the world's elite."

But what made the entire fiasco more striking in retrospect was the National Enquirer's publisher, American Media Inc., had its own mysterious close ties to Saudi Arabia. Six months before Jamal

Khashoggi's controversial murder, AMI published a shocking, high-quality glossy magazine for the many widely accused of being behind Khashoggi's murder, Mohammed bin Salmon. The print run was more than 200,000 copies and retailed for $13.99. It was essentially a p.r. extravaganza for bin Salman, showing photos of him with members of the world's powerful elite, including Bill Gates, Vladimir Putin, Xi Jimping, Shinzo Abe and five photos of President Trump. The bizarre special edition was available on every newsstand, supermarket, pharmacy, Walmart and airport across the U.S. Many news organizations were appalled that AMI would promote a notorious dictator like bin Salman in such a favorable light. Rumors spread quickly that financially strapped AMI did it for money, raising serious speculation that the Saudis financed the entire project.

"There's no other explanation that makes sense," a former AMI editor said. "The Enquirer and all of AMI was struggling financially for several years. By doing the bin Salman promotional magazine there were rumblings in the newsroom at AMI amongst many staffers that the entire thing was a complete sham. The conclusion many people drew was that the Saudis most likely paid for it handsomely. If that's the case, it was a clever, sleazy and shameless way for AMI to profit and to help inject much-needed cash into the struggling company."

But the story about Khashoggi's controversial murder goes much further. Multiple sources close to Epstein detailed how Epstein provided his powerful friend MBS with extensive secret files on Khashoggi, which included every private aspect of his life, and also his career as a journalist. One source claimed MBS paid Epstein millions of dollars in return, and full time residency in The Kingdom of Saudi Arabia.

"If not for Epstein I strongly believe Khashoggi would be alive today," a former close associate of Epstein said. "Epstein hired people to dig up everything on Khashoggi months before he was killed. He did it as a favor to his powerful friend, the Saudi Prince. He knew the Prince would pay him back handsomely for his work. Epstein was a snake, loyalty meant nothing to him. He'd rat out his own mother to make an extra buck. I know for a fact Epstein received millions from MBS for providing him high level secret information about Khashoggi, Israel, and corporate America."

I could see from the window at Benash how the sun peeked out but then hid behind the incoming Manhattan fog. An hour passed, then another and another. My interview with Epstein seemed like it would never end. Epstein forced his lips into a smile when I brought up the subject of his international business connections. "I do business all over the world," he told me. "The world's most powerful people take my calls. They love being around me."

I asked Epstein why they enjoy being around him so much. He was forthright. "I make them richer and I'm always surrounded by beautiful models," he replied. I pressed him further, asking him if he procures sex for them. "Off the record, strictly off the record," he said. "Of course. It's the best way to get them to loosen up. Sex sells, it's the oldest trade. I fix them up with famous and not so famous models who would never give them the time of day. But because I arrange it they are able to taste the best women in the world. I just fix them up. What goes on in the bedroom is none of my business. I don't ask questions but most of them end up fucking the girls for money. One prominent Libyan son of a famous politician once paid one of the world's top models $500,000 in a suitcase to spend a week with him on his yacht. I was the person who arranged it. Models make more money fucking around than they do strutting their hips on the runways."

The Libyan politician's son Epstein referred to was the son of the longtime Libyan leader Muammar Gaddafi. Saif al-Islam Gaddafi was the one time heir apparent to his notorious dictator father. He was introduced to Epstein by none other than Prince Andrew, who was longtime close friends with Gaddafi and his son. Prince Andrew visited Gaddafi's son in Libya on multiple occasions and embarked on several business deals together. Andrew was eager to get his longtime financial adviser and business partner Epstein involved in the action.

The three shared another passion that excited them more than anything else - young, beautiful women. Two former Buckingham Palace insiders confirmed that Gaddafi arranged young, beautiful girls for both Andrew and Epstein when they visited him in Libya's capital city, Tripoli. "Andrew visited Libya several times for two major reasons," a former Buckingham Palace employee revealed. "He wanted to business with Gaddafi's so he could make millions on oil deals with them, and he also wanted to shag as many young Libyan girls as he could. And the Gaddafi's were more than willing to oblige. They treated Andrew like a king, putting him up at Gaddafi's mansion and providing him with as many Libyan beauties as he could handle. Andrew developed an addiction for Libyan women and kept going back for more."

A former Epstein associate insists that Epstein exchanged secrets about Israel to the Gaddafi family in exchange for sex with underage Libyan girls. "Jeffrey visited Tripoli a few times and became a close ally of the Gadaffi family," he said. "The bugger turned out to be a mole. He exchanged with them all the secret intelligence he was given by the Mossad to them in exchange for underage Libyan virgins. Jeffrey boasted all the time about how many girls lost their virginity to him. He slept with many Libyan girls in exchange for all the secrets he shared with the Gadaffi's. He double-crossed everyone for sex, money and power.

Clearly, Epstein emerged as a spy for three major international powers - Saudi Arabia, Israel and

Libya. He turned top classified information to each one in exchange for favors - financial, sexual and under-the-table mega cash deals. He played each country in the palm of his hand. When he was asked by either of the three nations to do any favor he spared no humiliation. He felt obligated to fulfill. And make no mistake about it, the deranged sociopath went above and beyond to deliver.

"Jeffrey loved being around wealth and power," Claude Pepe said. "When world players asked him for a favor regarding money or getting them beautiful girls he always came through, usually delivering much more than they expected. And they were more than willing to pay him a hefty price for his services, often in the millions."

CHAPTER XIII - THE KING OF POP & THE KING OF ALL MEDIA

Epstein smiled at a woman who cruised by us wearing thigh-high boots and what must have been five pounds of deftly knotted and twisted gold chains around her neck. He commented about her hyper-Botoxed face.

"Stupid," he said. "Women lose their sex appeal when they do that because they start to look like mannequins. They end up hating themselves, when they do that it's a form of self-mutilation. That's why I like to be around younger women, they are natural and have no agenda. They are a nod to purity and sheer beauty."

More than five hours had passed since the interview started, and I was feeling if not calm, then some similar approximation of it. Epstein's head snapped around like a rubber band when a tall transgender woman walked by us and took a seat at a table adjacent to ours. For a few seconds, Epstein stared for a few seconds at the long haired, six-foot decked out black beauty. She looked back at him before Epstein turned away.

"I don't get it," he said. "Today's generation can't even figure out if they're a man or woman. Look at Michael Jackson, he was so handsome back in the day. Today he looks like a cross between Diana Ross and his sister Janet. He's had so many surgeries that have made him almost unrecognizable." After he mentioned The King of Pop, Epstein's head started throbbing and seemed to get a bit queasy. For one intense moment I was convinced he was about to confess something very disturbing about Michael. Epstein almost reflexively went into a dissertation about the legendary singer.

"I met him a couple of times and there's something about him I noticed that is gnawing at him," Epstein said. "It's as if he lives a life shrouded by deep inner secrets."

An awkward silence ensued before Epstein continued on. "I slightly hate myself for saying this but I know for a fact Michael is not a pedophile. I've met him and I know people close to him. I also followed the charges several years ago brought on by Jordan Chandler. They were bogus. I have talked to people close to him in his camp, and they told me Michael was forced to settle and not drag it out cause it would have been career suicide. I'd bet every dollar I have that Michael never molested young boys. Certainly he's eccentric and acts weird but I know for a fact he doesn't like young boys. Simply, it's just not who he is."

Epstein didn't flinch when he suggested Jackson might have been gay. "Who knows?", he said. "If he's not into young boys than he might be into older men. That makes more sense. He had fallen into a routine for years of being a man of mystery. All the women he dated seemed to be just to appease the fans and the people in the music industry. But deep inside Michael there's something very disturbing. He's been trying to deal with his inner demons for years. He had a rough childhood and was physically abused by his father Joe. That's the reason why his appearance looks so different today. He wants to rid himself of the Jackson DNA. He doesn't want to look like the rest of his family because of all the abuse he withstood when he was growing up."

Epstein proved to have some incredibly good foresight and assessment of Jackson inner personal life. Perhaps that was the nature of his business, dealing for decades in the financial industry, when half the people buy a stock, thinking it will up, and the other half sell the same stock, thinking it will tank. "You got to pay attention to the world going on around you," he told me. "When it comes to Michael I know more than most people. I've met him and I know people closely connected to him. It's very clear that something is off. He's keeping his personal secrets from the rest of the world, many who false label him a pedophile. All he has to do is come out and clear everything up. But for some reason he chooses not to."

I am no stranger to the world of Michael Jackson. Years later, in 2007, I set out to prove that Jackson was a child molester who had preyed on children for years. After a year-long investigation, which even saw me infiltrate Jackson's camp as an undercover hairdresser's assistant - I could find no evidence to support the child molestation allegations against him. Instead, I found numerous inconsistencies in the stories of the two boys who had previously accused Jackson of molestation. When I finally published my book, Unmasked, in 2009, the investigation centered instead on the events that led to Michael's early death - placing the blame squarely on greed and exploitation by Jackson's handlers. The book was an immediate sensation and rocketed to number one on the New York Times bestseller list. It also gave me important gravitas as a commentator on Jackson's life and death as I appeared on TV shows throughout the world.

Years later, in the winter of 2019, explosive allegations against Michael at the heart of a new documentary Finding Neverland surfaced. The allegations sounded instantly familiar to me because I was already familiar with both accusers - Wade Robson and James Safechuck - from my earlier investigation. Both men, now grown adult men, appeared on camera to describe in graphic detail how Jackson groomed them and molested them for years while earning the trust of their families. Their testimony was both heartbreaking and very convincing. To me, however, a lot of their words sounded suspiciously like those of the two previously discredited victims - Gavin Orvizo and Jordie Chandler - who had come forward years earlier with child molestation allegations against Michael. That could mean one of two things. Either the men were all telling the truth and their stories represented a pattern that suggested Jackson's guilt. Or they were lying in order to extort a share of the singer's multi-billion-dollar estate.

Both men, however, claimed that they were not interested in money and had only sued to embolden other abuse victims to come forward. It is these words that set off alarm bells for me and reminded me of the previous victims whose dubious claims were show to have almost certainly been motivated by money all along. Deciding to dig deeper into the court records, I discovered some very telling evidence that appeared to contradict the men's claims of selflessness. The records revealed that shortly before Robson made public his 2013 lawsuit, he had in fact filed the suit under a court seal and then approached the Jackson estate demanding a financial settlement accompanied by a non-disclosure agreement. It was only after the estate refused payout that he went public. The lawsuit had, in fact, followed a previous attempt to cash in. Robson had been shopping a tell-all book to publishers a year earlier detailing his abuse, but he received no offers.

Meanwhile, Safechuck's own credibility can be gauged by examining the story he told in his own lawsuit. Under oath, he claims that he only remembered that he had been abused in 2013 when he turned on the tv and saw Robson talking about his molestation. But in the film and subsequent interviews promoting Finding Neverland, Safechuck told a very different story. He claimed that he knew he had been abused as far back as 2005 and that's why he refused to testify on Jackson's behalf in the Gavin Arvizo trial.

It is another of Safechuck's claims form the lawsuit, in fact, that has already raised questions about the credibility of his allegations and the film itself. In depositions, he claimed that the abuse had come to an end in 1992. In the film, however, he goes into graphic details about how Jackson had abused him in the second story of the Neverland Train Station in a chamber that Safechuck described as the "rape room." After the film appeared, however, a British journalist uncovered evidence that the Neverland Train Station was only built in 1994 long after their relationship had ended. When this was publicly revealed, the film's director admitted that there were discrepancies in Safechuck's timeline but insisted that the evidence still supported the bulk of the man's claims.

During the course of my original investigation, I interviewed scored of experts on pedophilia and sexual abuse. A decade later, I contacted many of them again for their opinions on the latest allegations. The results are telling. A number wondered why so few victims went public in the years after Jackson's death. "If Jackson was the serial pedophile that is alleged, we would expect dozens, more like hundreds, of victims to have come forward with claims against the estate," said one internationally renowned Los Angeles psychiatrist who specializes in childhood trauma. "If anybody had a legitimate claim, it would have been a license to print money. We saw this when the scandal over the Catholic clergy surfaced, resulting in billions of dollars in settlements. Jackson had access to thousands of children, and ample opportunity, yet where are all the victims?"

Another Chicago-based expert echoed these doubts. "Jackson had access to god knows how many children over the years, probably an unlimited number. In a typical case, the perpetrator is unable to control his urges. So we would conclude that Jackson's victims would have to be a very high number. There would be a lot of victims out there eager to tell their stories after he passed away, possibly to set the record straight about this iconic figure, possibly to get themselves a payout. Whatever the motivation, this didn't happen. It's been ten years, I simply don't believe they are out there and I'm one of those who used to be convinced that Michael Jackson was a pedophile and a very sick man." She and a number of other pointed to the infamous case of the British broadcaster Jimmy Savile. Within a year after his 2011 death, hundreds of victims had come forward, leading police to label the once beloved BBC personality a "predatory sex offender."

I discovered crucial information about the state of Robson and Safechuck's personal lives and crumbling finances around the time that they came forward with their accusations. I also interviewed numerous friends and associated who cast doubt on both men's stories. Therefore, unwaveringly I exonerate Jackson from the accusations that threaten to erase his legacy. I blame his arrogance rather than naivete for ignoring the years of warnings from friends and family about his relationships with children and the public optics. Robson and Safechuck falsely tried to trumpet their shocking allegations at the heart of the film to awaken a sleeping ghost that was awakened from a nearly decade-long slumber. Sadly, Jackson was not able to defend himself against the sensationalist allegations because he had been dead since June 2010.

Epstein rattled on, trying to impress me about how much he knew about Jackson before switching back to Howard Stern. "You know I have to admit I was skeptical when I decided to meet you," he told me with a wide grin. "But this has been somewhat therapeutic for me."

The lunch was surprising relaxed, far more so than I had imagined. Epstein did fly back into high gear when he started talking again about Stern, providing penetrating insights into the personal and professional life of the enigmatic radio legend. Long before his celebrated run at Sirius, Epstein argued that Stern's considerable talents were often overshadowed by his outsized personality and that he didn't get the credit he deserved as a broadcast pioneer on par with Barbara Walters.

"No matter what nobody will ever take him seriously because he's somewhat of a bipolar personality," Epstein mused. "One day he has women taking off everything in his studio, and he's inspecting their pussies and the next day he's interviewing a Hollywood celebrity trying to be taken seriously. Nobody in the business operated like that except Howard. It makes him look somewhat of a lost soul, looking for attention and trying to appease everyone. It's amazing how his fan base has put up with him for so long. He's so complex and battles so many inner demons every day of his life. If anyone in the entertainment has led a secret life, certainly it's Howard. That's why he's been in therapy for so many years. He's a man of many personalities and nobody knows, including himself, which one will show up on air each day. He's getting paid millions for being a narcissist, lost soul on the airwaves. It's very concerning."

Like Jackson, Epstein boldly predicted Stern's future practically spot on. He told me Stern would end up having a net worth of one billion dollars and would leave CBS to join a "more progressive" media outlet. A few years after I interviewed Epstein, Stern did just that when he joined Sirius. His contract vested most of his money in the shares of Sirius XM. Much of the company's stock value stemmed from his association with the satellite network. "If Howard leaves, the stock price would collapse and so would Howard's massive wealth," a Sirius insider told me. "It's the ultimate catch-22 and a giant albatross around his neck."

CHAPTER XIV - WHO
KILLED JEFFREY EPSTEIN?

Finally, our lengthy interview was coming to an end. Before he stepped up, Epstein insisted on paying the check. He took out a twenty dollar bill and put it in the hands of the waitress. "This is for you. Great service," he said. "You're the best. This is for you darling." Putting his hands on his hips, he struck a pose of deeply aggrieved authority. For a full two minutes he stood there until I said, "Thank you for coming and thanks for all the information you gave me. You certainly shed a lot of light."

Epstein's voice was tranquil, somewhat subdued as he said, "remember, everything I told you is off the record. If you use it please attribute it to an unnamed source. I presume you will respect that." Epstein then put his arm around me, and looked told me in a most serious tone, "when I die feel free to use it on the record. It will clear a lot up about who Jeffrey Epstein is. There are people who'd love to see me dead, people who want to kill me. So when I die you have my full permission to attribute it to me."

I adhered to his wishes until he died. But as I delved deeper and deeper into Epstein's atrocious life habits, I felt the time had come to dig up my old notes and conversations with him and let the world know what he revealed to me that dark November day back in 2001. To this day I'm still in shock at the abuse, violence and criminal activity that had overtaken the sociopath's life. I could feel the terror and the panic of the immense Epstein mantra as it tore through his victims, like a boat ripping through the ocean with the blade driven into its flanks. It had to be like some new species of death and darkness that Epstein fashioned fear for its leisure.

Years later, I realized how fortunate I was to get a one-on-one with the noted sociopath, who rarely gave media interviews. Epstein was notoriously tight guarded and ran an extremely tight ship to protect him from being outed. Many people I interviewed explained to me how frustrated they became by Epstein's lack of cooperation.

"He would have been shut down and gone to jail many years earlier if things leaked out," Claude Pepe revealed. "Somehow he was able to buy everyone's silence. Look at what happened with the Quebec businessmen and politician who visited his private island many times. They could have gone back and told the authorities about all the underage girls on his island. But they didn't because Epstein got them involved. In fact, they would could have gone to jail to. They were so deeply involved in everything Epstein offered them, including underage girls, drugs and wild orgies."

The last time I spoke to Pepe, he went into shocking detail about how Epstein once pondered killing former French President Nicolas Sarkozy. Pepe explained how Epstein began a decade long infatuation with supermodel Carla Bruni a couple years after his previous obsession Princess Diana died in a car crash. Pepe said Epstein thought Bruni was the most beautiful woman in the world and collected hundreds of photos of her. When the famous supermodel began dating Sarkozy in 2007, Epstein went berserk.

"He plotted on killing Sarkozy before the wedding which took place in February 2008, a few months after Bruni and Sarkozy started dating. I know for a fact Epstein was looking to hire a professional hitman in Paris to take out Sarkozy. He went completely insane. He wanted to destroy Sarkozy for "stealing" Bruni, even though he never dated her."

Pepe insists Epstein got back at Sarkozy by alerting French police how Sarkozy allegedly took a huge amount of cash from Libyan leader Muammar Gaddafi for his 2007 presidential campaign. As detailed in a previous chapter, Epstein was close to the former Libyan dictator and his son, carrying out several acts of espionage for them in exchange for beautiful, underage Libyan girls.

"Gaddafi told Epstein how he gave Sarkozy almost 50 million euros," Pepe said. "They were very close friends. They used to speak regularly. Epstein was so jealous of Sarkozy that he had a close associate go to French authorities and rat out Sarkozy. He once told me he hopes Sarkozy goes to jail forever for stealing his "woman". He was completely out of his mind most of the time, but when it came to Bruni he was insane. He said he'd do everything in his power to bury Sarkozy."

"Saturday, August 10, 2019, at approximately 6.30am, inmate Jeffrey Edward Epstein was found unresponsive in his cell ... subsequently pronounced dead by hospital staff," read a statement from the Metropolitan Correctional Center where Epstein, 66, had been held without bail since he was arrested on July 6th on charges of sex trafficking girls as young as 14.

News outlets around the world quickly reported Epstein died by suicide. The FBI confirmed it was investigating Epstein's death, and the attorney general, William Barr, said he had also opened an investigation by the Department of Justice's inspector general and was "appalled" by the death. "Epstein's death raises serious questions that must be answered," Barr said. Barr said there were "serious irregularities" at the jail where Epstein was held.

The same day Epstein died, more than 2,000 pages of court documents in his case were finally unsealed after a court order. The documents revealed that one of Epstein's underage victims, Virginia Roberts Giuffre, swore under oath in 2016 that Epstein ordered her to have sex with some of the world's most powerful and famous people. They have all denied Giuffre's explosive allegations.

"I believe Jeffrey was killed because to silence him from incriminating other powerful people involved in his elaborate sex trafficking ring," a former Epstein employee revealed. "If he was forced to testify he would have outed a lot more people. Somebody killed him to avoid all that. Jeffrey was a twisted man, nobody can deny it. But he was a person who always fought to the end, even if he was guilty. He was also a person who was proud, had a massive ego and loved life. I guarantee you he would never commit suicide or even think about it. Simply, it was not who he was and no matter how bad things got he just couldn't entertain the thought."

Epstein's death came just days after he was found unconscious in a Manhattan jail cell with injuries to his neck, media outlets had reported, citing numerous anonymous sources. It was not clear how he suffered those injuries. Two anonymous sources told New York's local NBC News4 that Epstein's injuries may have been self-inflicted, while another said an assault by another inmate had not been ruled out. Immediately following the incident, Epstein had been placed on suicide watch.

Within minutes of the breaking news, my phone started ringing off the hook. E-mails began to pour in Most of them demanded to know the same thing: Was Jeffrey Epstein's death really suicide? Was he murdered?

I didn't give much thought to the claims until a few hours later, when I got a call from Epstein's former associate Claude Pepe. Pepe provided me some damning testimony. "There's no way he committed suicide," Pepe told me. "Jeffrey intended to fight the new sex trafficking charges vigorously. He believed the new charges was an entire set-up to take him down because he knew too much about famous people like Bill Clinton, Prince Andrew and many others. I also believe Ghislaine Maxwell threw him under the bus to the feds, providing them with a lot of information when she was deposed a few years ago. Many of the people who were connected him wanted him rubbed out. If there's one thing I know for sure is that Jeffrey would never in a million years commit suicide. He loved himself too much, and he loved life. I guarantee this was a most professional job."

In the days and months after Epstein's death, the murder theory took on an unstoppable momentum of its own. Several new crucial pieces of evidence had surfaced, and I came into some damning new evidence of my own, including a phone call I received from a former top Buckingham Palace official who insisted Epstein's death was linked to his involvement with Prince Andrew.

"I know you're writing a book about Epstein's death," he told me. "I can tell you that if Prince Andrew wasn't so deeply involved with Epstein I believe he'd still be alive. The British Royal Family is the most powerful organization in the world. They can pull off whatever they want, whatever is needed to do to protect them." I asked the former official if he was insinuating that the Queen played a hand in Epstein's death. His response sent chills down my spine. "The Queen doesn't involve herself in such matters," he said. "But Prince Philip is a monster and can orchestrate whatever he wants. He's a dirty, dangerous old man. I know for a fact he didn't shed any tears the day Epstein was found dead. In fact, I was told first hand he breathed a sigh of relief." I asked the official if Epstein's death conjured up images of Princess Diana's tragic death, when her lover's billionaire father Mohamed Al-Fayed accused the Royal Family and Prince Philip of murder.

"It's different," he said. "I do believe Prince Philip and others wanted Fayed's son Dodi killed. The last thing they wanted was for Diana to marry an Egyptian Muslim. It would have brought them irreparable shame, so they thought. Epstein was much different. They feared for their lives and for the future of the monarchy that Epstein would out Andrew for sleeping with underage girls. I know for a fact they wanted Epstein killed. I have corroboration on that. It was the only way to guarantee his silence would be forever."

Another longtime Epstein friend and associate insisted his friend wasn't suicidal, even though he was facing a potential life sentence if he was convicted of the most recent charges. He said he spoke to a very upbeat Epstein a couple days before his arrest July 6, 2019 at Teterboro Airport in New Jersey after his private jet landed there from Paris. Teterboro Airport was long labeled the travel hub of Epstein's sex traffic ring, where his fleet of private planes logged at least 730 flights to and from Teterboro between 1995 and 2013 delivering hundreds of sex slaves to notorious celebrities, politicians, businessmen and royals.

"Jeffrey owned many different private jets," Claude Pepe said. "He'd put the young sex slaves on the plane, would have people on the plane to groom them properly with manicures, pedicures and facials so that they'd look good and be ready to perform for the high profile people that they would be hooked up with on his private island or his ranch in New Mexico. They were paid for hire and were forced to perform whatever sexual acts they were asked to do."

New York City Chief Medical Examiner Dr. Barbara Sampson ruled that Epstein died of suicide by hanging and rejected conspiracy theories that foul play was involved. For years to come, murder theorists will argue against Sampson's conclusion. However, several key people close to Epstein and forensic pathological experts are intent to contradict Sampson, providing key information that contradicts Sampson, making her findings look unthorough and extremely presumptuous. It's hard to deny that

Epstein was a troubled soul, but it's not outside the realm of possibility that he was murdered.

The first key person to cast doubt on the Epstein's alleged suicide was his defense lawyer, who expressed deep skepticism that the wealthy financier hanged himself in a Manhattan federal jail while awaiting trial on the new charges. He claimed that the injuries suffered by Epstein were more common in strangulation than in hanging.

"Far more consistent with assault," lawyer Reid Weingarten told Judge Richard Berman in U.S. District Court in Manhattan during a hearing to weigh the merits of dismissing the child sex trafficking charges against Epstein because he had died. Weingarten told the judge that when he and other members of Epstein's legal defense team spoke to Epstein shortly before his death that he was very positive and showed no signs of contemplating suicide. "We did not see a despairing, despondent, suicidal person," he told the judge. "We want the court to help us find out what happened. We're skeptical of the certitude. There are significant doubts regarding the conclusion of suicide."

Another Epstein lawyer, Martin Weinberg, told Judge Berman that the conditions Epstein was subjected to while being incarcerated were "horrific and medieval". He told the judge that there was a strong possibility Epstein was murdered in his jail cell, and did not commit suicide. Reid Weingarten corroborated Weinberg's claims about how Epstein was subjected to subhuman conditions. "In a word, they were dreadful," he told Berman. "There was vermin, standing water and lack of natural light."

Defense lawyer Weingarten went further, telling the judge that he had heard from several key people that the surveillance video at the jail around Epstein's cell had been disconnected. "They were either corrupted or not functioning," Weingarten said. The cameras Weingarten alluded to were sent to the FBI crime lab in Quantico, Virginia for examination. The crime lab in Virginia is a major facility where agents and forensic scientists dissect and analyze evidence.

Furthermore, it was revealed that two jail guards failed to follow a procedure overnight to conduct separate checks on Epstein every 30 minutes. The two federal prison officers, Tova Noel and Michael Thomas, were assigned to Epstein's special housing unit at the Metropolitan Correctional Center. They were charged with falsifying records, stating they had checked on Epstein in the hours before he hanged himself, and browsing the internet in a common area and falling asleep for two hours when they should have been carrying out inmate checks.

"Smells very fishy, someone got paid well to set this up," said a former FBI agent who has followed the Epstein saga for years. "Too many high profile people stood to lose a lot if Epstein was forced to testify under oath. A lot of lives would have been ruined forever. I worked on cases like this for more than twenty years. It's very clear to me that someone wanted Epstein dead and ordered him to be taken out. The cameras not working, and the very suspicious, negligent behaviour of the prison guards all adds up to only one verdict - Epstein was a lame duck. Someone with a lot of power ordered him to be taken out."

Lawmakers expressed deep concern over the security breakdown surrounding Epstein's death. Senator Ben Sasse (R-Nebraska) labeled Epstein's death "a crisis of public trust" within the prison system. "You are in this job because of this crisis," Sasse told Kathleen Hawk Sawyer, who was put in charge by Attorney General William Barr at the federal Bureau of Prisons in a shakeup as a result of the negligence surrounding Epstein's death. "That bastard now won't be able to testify against his other co-conspirators. Heads needed to roll the day Jeffrey Epstein died. The Bureau of Prisons and the Department of Justice need to start giving the public some answers. These arrests are important, but they're not the end of this. These guards aren't the only ones who should stand trial - every one of Jeffrey Epstein's co-conspirators should be spending the rest of their lives behind bars."

Hawk Sawyer said she was not permitted to comment on the ongoing criminal trial of the guards but acknowledged the system had failed providing proper surveillance on Epstein. "We don't want those people working in federal prisons," she said. "This incident was a black eye on the entire Bureau of Prisons. We have some bad staff; we want to get rid of bad staff. The only time we ever noticed is when something bad happens."

"I don't buy their excuses," the former FBI agent who worked on similar type cases said. "When you have a high profile person like Epstein in jail nothing is supposed to go wrong. And it won't go wrong unless there an intentional screw up, which is what I believe happened in this particular case. It was a most professional job, people who knew what they were doing came in and disconnected the cameras, knocked out the guards with sleeping gas and then took care of Epstein. It's the only plausible explanation in this particular case. I can't accept any other theory. It's impossible that Epstein wasn't intentionally taken out. Strange things like this just don't happen in jail, especially when it comes to high profile inmates. I've worked in law enforcement my entire life. One thing I learned is that if people high up want someone taken out it can be done very easily."

Perhaps the biggest bombshell to drop was the murky events surrounding the mysterious circumstances of Epstein's alleged first suicide, the incident with his cellmate weeks before he died. In late December 2019, just days after confirming they were unable to locate surveillance video captured outside Epstein's cell on the night of his alleged first suicide attempt, prosecutors told a federal judge the video was finally retrieved. The video purportedly showed the exterior of the MCC jail cell that Epstein shared with Nicholas Tartaglione, a former police office who faced possible death-penalty in a quadruple murder. Taraglione's defense lawyer Bruce Barket had requested the footage two days after the July 23 incident but was told it was missing. Months later it finally surfaced.

"We are very pleased the video was preserved, as we had asked," Barket said. "We look forward to viewing it." In a letter later that day, Assistant U.S. Attorneys Maurene Comey (daughter of former FBI director James Comey) and Jason Swergold told District Judge kenneth M. Karas that the footage had finally been found. "Earlier today, the government confirmed with MCC staff that the video was preserved by MCC staff upon defense counsel's request in July 2019, and the government is in the process of obtaining a copy of the video," the prosecutors said a one-page statement.

Less than a month later on January 9, 2020 the mystery surrounding the video deepened when it was revealed that the contents on the tape were permanently deleted as "a result of technical errors." It joined a long list of bizarre incidents surrounding Epstein's death and imprisonment.

Assistant U.S. Attorney Swergold and Comey this time filed a letter that contradicted the one-page statement they had made a month earlier. "The footage contained on the preserved video was for the correct date and time, but captured a different tier than the one where Cell-1 was located," they wrote. "The requested video no longer exists on the backup system and has not since at least August 2019 as a result of technical errors."

Incredibly, the backup system the MCC had also failed. Technical errors were cited for being the reason why the backup recording was deleted. A review by the FBI found that the video was on the backup but was deleted in August 2019 due to technical errors.

"This is completely unacceptable," the former FBI agent said. "It has cover up written all over it. Never in my 30-year career have I ever heard of backup tapes being deleted. In my mind someone erased those tapes on purpose. It's a felony to do it and the people who did it were ordered by someone very high up to delete all the tapes. Those people should be held accountable and charged. And they should be forced to reveal who ordered the murder of Jeffrey Epstein."

Finally, almost three months after Epstein died, the world learned from a top private pathologist that it was not an open-and-shut case of suicide. Dr. Michael Baden, hired by Epstein's brother Mark, strongly disputed the official autopsy, claiming that Epstein did not commit suicide but appeared to have been strangled. Dr. Baden described how Epstein sustained a number of serious injuries that would have killed him, including a broken bone in his neck. "They are extremely unusual in suicidal hangings and could occur much more commonly in homicidal strangulation," he said on the morning TV show

"Fox&Friends". "I think the evidence points to homicide rather than suicide. I've not seen in 50 years where that occurred in a suicidal hanging case."

Dr. Baden was present for the autopsy conducted by city officials after Epstein was found dead. If anyone was an expert on autopsies it certainly was Dr. Baden, who performed more than 20,000 during his storied career, earning a reputation as one of the world's foremost forensic pathologists. He was featured in an HBO special about his work and was involved in some of world's the highest profile death investigations, including the assassination of President John F. Kennedy. Dr. Baden also served as New York City's medical examiner and earned a reputation for being an expert on how crime scenes within the confines of jails and prisons are sometimes tampered with.

Dr. Baden described how Epstein the injuries suffered were critical to the case. "He had three fractures in the hyoid bone, the thyroid cartilage," he said. "Those injuries were very unusual for suicide and more indicative of strangulation - homicidal strangulation."

Dr. Barbara Sampson, the person who ruled Epstein's August 10th death in his jail cell was a suicide, was quick to try to discredit Dr. Baden's findings.

"I stand firmly behind our determination of the cause and manner of death in this case," Sampson said.

"In general, fractures of the hyoid bone and the cartilage can be seen in suicides and homicides." She insisted her office carried out a "complete investigation", based on information provided to her by law enforcement.

Dr. Baden pointed out how suspicious it was that no photo exists of Epstein's body as it was found in his jail cell. A top forensic pathologist said that the key to determining whether it was suicide or murder would be to be aware of the exact position of in which Epstein was found.

"Without it there's no way of really knowing what happened," he said. "Any credible medical professional would keep cause of death undetermined until this information was known. Without knowing the location of the ligature around his neck, the exact injuries on his body and the way the blood pooled after his death it would be impossible and very irresponsible to determine the cause of death."

Dr. Baden agreed. He told 60 Minutes: "At this length of time we still don't have that information. So if this was called a suicide without all that information, it was a premature judgment."

Dr. Baden also pointed out how Epstein had hemorrhages in his eyes when he died, something much more likely to occur in strangulation than hanging.

More damning were the questions raised about whether the correct ligature was examined in Epstein's hanging. Several contradictory theories about the ligature have made the rounds since Epstein's death, including that the authorities tampered with the evidence on the scene.

Police photos of the scene revealed at least two nooses were found on the floor of Epstein's cell. Both were made from strips of orange bedsheets. Raising more concerns was that the photos of the noose taken in as evidence showed no cuts and was neatly folded and hemmed. Multiple sources connected to the case insist the guard who discovered Epstein's dead body cut the ligature before trying resuscitate him. If that's the case , many forensic experts will argue it's practically impossible that Epstein committed suicide.

"There were no cuts on the noose," one New York law enforcement source admitted. "Nobody ever tried to cut it. So it appears they examined the wrong noose. The question is why? Were they intent on covering it all up to make it look like a suicide? There's a very strong possibility that's exactly what happened. Too many famous people would have had all the gory details about their relationship with Epstein revealed if he didn't die. I've investigated hundreds of suicides during my career. This one appears to have too many key aspects pointing in another direction - an intentional homicide. After examining all the key elements and evidence in the case, I conclude there's no other sensible explanation. Epstein was most likely taken out by professional killers who are still at large. The chance of them ever being brought to justice is less likely than OJ Simpson finding the real killers of Nicole Brown Simpson. I guarantee you it will never happen."

Some medical experts argue that multiple

neck fractures do not automatically give a homicide verdict. CNN Chief Medical Correspondent Dr. Sanjay Gupta contradicted Dr. Baden's prognosis.

"In strangulation, while you can break the hyoid bone, it is less likely to actually break bones in the neck," Gupta said. "By hanging, someone can break both the hyoid bone and other bones in the neck. None of these factors in isolation give you a complete story."

More than a year after Epstein's death, there were still no answers from the federal Bureau of Prisons on how he really died after a promised investigation and a call for more transparency. "We will get to the bottom of it, and there will be accountability," Attorney General William Barr guaranteed shortly after Epstein died. Barr would later rule out murder, claiming he had reviewed the surveillance footage and was certain nobody had gained entry to Epstein's cell before he died. What he didn't mention was that Epstein was dead for three hours before he was found dead. To this day Barr has remained vague on how much of the footage he was able to view, as it was revealed that most of the footage had somehow been damaged and unable to view.

"I can understand people who immediately, whose minds went to sort of the worst-case scenario because it was a perfect storm of screw-ups," Barr told the Associated Press.

One person who was close to Epstein for years and seemed convinced there was foul play was none other than President Donald Trump. Trump was not shy to go against the suicide verdict spewed by medical experts and his attorney general.

"People are still trying to figure out how did it happen," Trump said in an interview with Axios. "Was it suicide? Was he killed?"

As the public and media demand answers about the actual cause of Epstein's death, authorities seem intent on dousing reports of anything other than a suicide verdict. No matter what the deranged man's actual cause of death was, Epstein was spared a prolonged trial that most likely would have sent him to prison for the rest of his life.

A former inmate at the jail perhaps shed the most light in a 60 Minutes interview. He said it was impossible for Epstein to kill himself with the bedsheet, because it was "paper level, not strong enough."

After interviewing several of the world's leading forensic pathologists who specialize in true crime stories, I conclude unwaveringly that Jeffrey Epstein was murdered. A combination of the bizarre behaviour of the prison guards, the injuries he suffered, the two ligatures found in his cell and the missing video surveillance footage likely add up to a professional inside hit. No matter what the fly on the walls in Epstein's jail cell witnessed when he died, it's certain that foul play was involved and his death is nothing short of one major coverup that authorities will most likely never get to the bottom of. More importantly, no matter how he died it in no way acquits the plethora of high profile people still roaming out there unscathed who bought into and supported his criminal lifestyle. Famous, wealthy enablers like Prince Andrew and Bill Clinton must be forced to disclose all the intricate details of their longstanding associations with one of the world's most notorious child sex traffickers. It might be the only way Epstein's victims and their families can ever get justice and some sort of closure. His victims deserve justice - not secrecy and sweet plea deals to the men who were enabled by Epstein to turn them into their sex slaves.

The good news is that Epstein's death does not in any way extinguish the hundreds of victims of his sex trafficking ring from receiving restitution. Although they might never get over the inhumane acts Epstein subjected them to, dozens of these courageous women have sued his estate and, if justice finally prevails, will walk away with huge financial settlements.

"That's the only good part of this," an Epstein victim told me in August 2020. "I wish he'd be alive to stand trial, so I could look at him in the eye when I testified on the stand. I wanted him to be found guilty and sent to prison forever. Truly, I believe he was murdered, so he would not be able to out all his famous friends like Bill Clinton and Prince Andrew.

It's a shame that the authorities are covering it all up. There are so many women out there like myself who were sexually abused by him and have suffered so much psychological damage and hurt for many years. Because he died, I don't think any of us will ever be able to have full closure, no matter how much money we receive."

◆ ◆ ◆

The media seem to have taken the allegations against Prince Andrew more seriously than ever before, but it still doesn't go about it in the way it should. Millions of girls are forced into illegal child sex trafficking every year. Many of them are subjected to inhumane conditions - beaten, raped and murdered. I'll always do my best to expose this disgusting form of treatment against innocent minor who are unwillingly brought into this. It's hard to find something more despicable and disturbing than child sex trafficking. Perhaps this book will help people comprehend how serious a problem it is and how important it is to expose such disturbing criminal activity. But the problem remains, unfortunately, by the time you catch one child sex trafficker like Jeffrey Epstein, 50 others have been trained in his place.

In January 2021, I received the most disturbing phone call of my entire investigation. The call lasted barely two minutes. An old contact of mine passed my number to a French woman named "Janice", who claimed she was raped by Epstein when she was 15 years old and had sex with Prince Andrew nine days before turning 18.

"I just want to confirm with you Ian that I was one of many girls Prince Andrew had sex with in Jeffrey Epstein's home. I was paid off to keep quiet years ago by Epstein.

"I was going to turn eighteen more than a week later after I had sex with Prince Andrew. He never asked me my age. I was drunk at Epstein's home on his private island when Andrew threw himself on me and forced me to have sex with him. To this day I can't believe how Prince Andrew has never been investigated or held accountable.

"The Royal Family is despicable. They launch investigations into poor Meghan Markle's behaviour when she lived in the United Kingdom, and try to destroy Prince Harry's marriage by taking away his royal status and security. But they refuse to launch an investigation into Prince Andrew, a man who is a walking predator. They have their priorities completely fucked up and I hope the authorities eventually step in and charge Prince Andrew for his unlawful behaviour." "Janice" refused to say more. "One day the entire truth will come out," she said. "Now is not the time because Andrew seems to be above the law. I promise, the final chapter of this sad saga is far from being written."

OFFICE OF CHIEF MEDICAL EXAMINER
CITY OF NEW YORK

REPORT OF AUTOPSY

Name of Decedent: Jeffrey Edward Epstein   M.E. #: M-19-019432

Autopsy Performed by: Kristin Roman, M.D.   Date of Autopsy: 08/11/2019

FINAL DIAGNOSES:

I. HANGING:
   A. LIGATURE FURROW OF NECK
   B. PETECHIAL HEMORRHAGES OF BILATERAL PALPEBRAL
      CONJUNCTIVAE AND OF ORAL MUCOSA
   C. CONFLUENT HEMORRHAGES OF RIGHT BULBAR CONJUNCTIVA
   D. PLETHORA OF FACE AND HEAD WITH PETECHIAL HEMORRHAGES OF
      FACE
   E. FRACTURES OF BILATERAL THYROID CARTILAGE CORNUAE AND
      LEFT HYOID CORNUA WITH ACCOMPANYING SOFT TISSUE
      HEMORRHAGES
      1. SEE ANTHROPOLOGY REPORT
   F. RESUSCITATION ATTEMPTED
      1. ABRASIONS OF MOUTH
      2. ANTERIOR PARASTERNAL RIB FRACTURES
      3. HEPATIC LACERATION WITH THIN HEMOPERITONEUM
II. ABRASIONS OF LEFT FOREARM
III. CUTANEOUS CONTUSIONS OF WRISTS
IV. SUBCUTANEOUS HEMORRHAGE OF LEFT DELTOID MUSCLE
V. HYPERTENSIVE AND ATHEROSCLEROTIC CARDIOVASCULAR DISEASE
   A. CARDIAC HYPERTROPHY (440 GM)
   B. LEFT VENTRICLE HYPERTROPHY (1.9 CM)
   C. RENAL ARTERIOLAR SCLEROSIS
   D. SLIGHT CORONARY ATHEROSCLEROSIS
   E. SLIGHT TO MODERATE AORTIC ATHEROSCLEROSIS
VI. HEPATIC STEATOSIS (2480 GM)
VII. CERVICAL LYMPHADENOPATHY
VIII. REMOTE FRACTURE OF RIGHT FIRST RIB
IX. REMOTE APPENDECTOMY (DATE AND INDICATION UNKNOWN)
X. SEE TOXICOLOGY REPORT
XI. SEE NEUROPATHOLOGY REPORT

The Door To Epstein's Cell After He Died

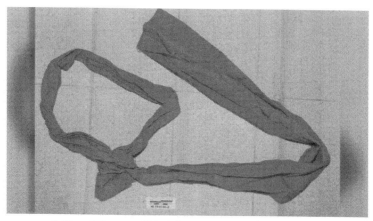

A Key Piece of Evidence Was The Noose

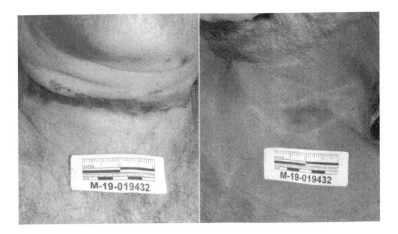

Epstein's Neck After He Was Found Dead

Epstein's Jail Cell At The Time Of His Death

UNITED STATES DISTRICT COURT
SOUTHERN DISTRICT OF NEW YORK

ELECTRONICALLY
DOC #:
DATE FILED: [illegible]

United States of America,

-v-

Ghislaine Maxwell,

Defendant.

20-CR-330 (AJN)

MEMORANDUM
OPINION & ORDER

ALISON J. NATHAN, District Judge:

Both parties have asked for the Court to enter a protective order. While they agree on most of the language, two areas of dispute have emerged. First, Ms. Maxwell seeks language allowing her to publicly reference alleged victims or witnesses who have spoken on the public record so the media or in public fora, or in litigation relating to Ms. Maxwell or Jeffrey Epstein. Second, Ms. Maxwell seeks language restricting potential Government witnesses and their counsel from using discovery materials for any purpose other than preparing for the criminal trial in this action. The Government has proposed contrary language on both of these issues. For the following reasons, the Court adopts the Government's proposed protective order.

Epstein's Longtime Partner Ghislaine Maxwell Faces A Huge Legal Battle. After Her Arrest She Pleaded Not Guilty, Contradicting Many Of The People Who Accused Her Of Procuring Underage Girls For Epstein.

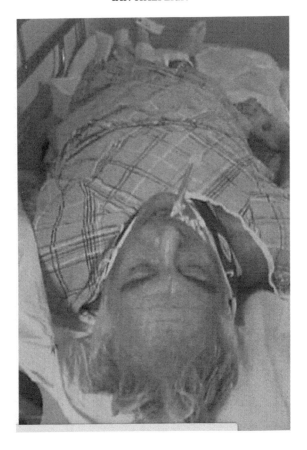

Epstein's Body The Morning Of His Death.

Thank you all for the incredible support. No names mentioned, but you know who you are.

To read more Ian Halperin books published recently, please go to Amazon and select:

Covid-19: Reflective Winds In the Deadly Corona

Keeping Secrets: Undercover In The Hollywood Closet

To view Ian Halperin's latest documentary film, please go to Amazon or Vimeoondemand and select:

Wish You Weren't Here: The Dark Side of Roger Waters

Printed in Great Britain
by Amazon